State of Visually Impaired in 75 Years of Independent India: Issues and Challenges

(A Collection of Articles)

Karna Vidya Foundation

Collected and Compiled by

Dr. K. Raghuraman

INDIA · SINGAPORE · MALAYSIA

ISBN
Paperback 979-8-89744-692-6
Hardcase 979-8-89777-284-1

Contents

Introduction	5
Acknowledgment	9
Finding Happiness In Sorrows Of Life	11
How I Approached Maths As A Visually Impaired Student	13
Gender And Disability	16
Journey of Visually Impaired Population in Independent India - Challenges & way forward	19
Champions Of Inner Light!	27
Scope Of Visually Challenged People In Banking Sector:	32
Why I Like The Temple (Poem)	35
Making Of A Specially Abled Doctor.	37
State of Visually Impaired in 75 Years of Independent India: Issues and Challenges	40
Navigating the intersection of Visual Impairment & Artificial Intelligence: A Deep Dive into Empowerment, Prospects & Future Challenges	44
Enhancing Spatial Awareness: For the Visually Impaired	53
Overcoming Barriers: My Journey as a Student with Visual Impairment in STEM Education	65
A Forgotten Blind Mathematician Of India: Story of Dr. Lakkoju Sanjeevarayalu, 22/11/1907 to 02/12/1997	68
Understanding Individuals With Visual Impairment	71
Towards Financial Inclusion for Persons with Visual Impairment: Addressing Ableism to Pave the Way for Barrier-Free Access to Banking and Other Financial Services	79
Karna Vidya Foundation	91

Introduction

At the outset, I wish to place on record my sincere appreciation to Karna Vidya Foundation for having compiled such a rich collection of articles pertaining to visual impairment and visually impaired people in the Indian context. This book is a welcome addition to the existing literature on disability, primarily for documenting the lived experience of blind individuals in different dimensions and with an immense range of socio-cultural perspectives. Vision impairment is not merely a biological condition, it is rather a lived experience deeply rooted in social reality, cultural phenomena and politico-economic conditions. Nature of vision impairments and varied sociocultural interactions resist any monolithic understanding of blindness. While documenting individual experiences and their success stories, this collection sets in motion several poignant conversations pertaining to vision impaired persons in India.

In the realm of disability studies, the concept of disability has undergone a profound shift, moving away from the medical model that places emphasis on impairment and towards the social model that highlights the disabling barriers imposed by society upon individuals with impairments. This paradigm shift underscores the significance of comprehending disability as a complex interplay of biological, social, and environmental factors. This understanding is crucial for inferring the true nuances about blindness and lives of vision impaired people in India.

The social model of disability posits that disability is not merely an individual's inherent condition, but rather a consequence of the social and environmental constraints that hinder their full participation in society. These disabling barriers can manifest in various forms, such as inaccessible infrastructure, discriminatory attitudes, and exclusionary practices. By recognizing the role of social factors in creating disability, the social model advocates for the removal of these barriers to enable individuals with impairments to exercise their rights and participate fully in society. This collection contributes to this mission of advocacy by disabled individuals and disabled persons' organizations (DPOs). Articles pertaining to the progress of vision impaired people in post-colonial India, as well as challenges and opportunities in law, mathematics, artificial intelligence, banking and finance sectors provide valuable inputs for furthering the cause of disability advocacy, enhancing accessibility and creating a more inclusive society.

The concept of intersectionality further enriches our understanding of disability by acknowledging the multiple and intersecting identities that individuals possess. Individuals are not solely defined by their disability but also by their gender, race, ethnicity, sexual orientation, and other social identities. These intersecting identities can create unique experiences of disability, as individuals may face multiple forms of discrimination and marginalization. For instance, women with blindness may encounter barriers related to both their gender and disability, resulting in compounded disadvantage. Articles in this collection bring out several intersectional factors like gender, technological knowledge, education, locality and economic position which contribute to the lives and experiences of blind individuals in India.

The notion of 'reasonable accommodation' is pivotal in ensuring that individuals with disabilities have equal opportunities to participate in society. Reasonable accommodation refers to the necessary and appropriate modifications and adjustments that enable individuals with disabilities to access education, employment, and other services on an equal basis with others. These accommodations can range from accessible infrastructure to assistive technologies and support services. The provision of reasonable accommodation is not merely a matter of goodwill but a legal obligation in many countries, including India, under the Rights of Persons with Disabilities Act (2016).

The significance of braille literacy in the lives of individuals with visual impairments cannot be overstated. Braille literacy empowers individuals to pursue education, secure employment, and participate fully in society. It fosters independence and self-reliance, enabling individuals to navigate their surroundings, access information, and engage in meaningful occupations.

The advent of artificial intelligence (AI) has ushered in both opportunities and challenges for individuals with visual impairments. AI-powered assistive technologies, such as screen readers, voice assistants, and object recognition apps, have the potential to enhance accessibility and empower individuals with vision loss. These technologies can facilitate access to information, communication, and navigation, enabling greater independence and participation in society. However, it is essential to address the potential biases and limitations of AI tools to ensure that they are inclusive and accessible to all individuals with visual impairments.

In the following few paragraphs, I shall delve into the diverse themes explored in the articles presented in this collection, to offer a glimpse into the valuable insights they offer.

Aastha Singhal, a chartered accountant who gradually lost her vision, shares her poignant journey of adapting to a world without sight in her article **"Finding Happiness in Sorrows of Life"**. She recounts the challenges she faced in completing her education, relying on the support of her family and friends. Singhal's story is a testament to the resilience manifested by thousands and thousands of vision impaired persons in India, as well as the transformative power of accepting blindness.

Abhishek Dhol, a law student who has been blind since the age of four, shares his experiences of studying mathematics as a visually impaired student in his lucidly written article **"How I Approached Maths As A Visually Impaired Student"**. He emphasizes the importance of accessibility, sustained application and practice, and a culture of high expectations in enabling visually impaired students to succeed in mathematics. Dhol's insights offer valuable guidance for educators and students alike in fostering inclusive education.

In her chapter titled **"Gender and Disability"**, Ambika Khattar, a PhD scholar, explores the intersectionality of gender and disability, focusing on the unique challenges faced by women and girls with disabilities. She discusses the historical denial of admission to inclusive schools for girls with disabilities and the heightened risk of sexual violence they face. Khattar's analysis sheds light on the urgent need to address the systemic inequalities that perpetuate the marginalization of women and girls with vision impairment.

Aravind Rajendran, a renowned banker and an optimistic person, discusses the scope of visually challenged people in the banking sector, highlighting the impact of technological advancements on employment opportunities. His article **"Scope Of Visually Challenged People In Banking Sector"** emphasizes the importance of continuous upskilling and adaptation to remain competitive in the evolving banking landscape. Aravind's insights offer valuable guidance for visually challenged individuals seeking to navigate the dynamic world of banking.

The essay **"Why I Like The Temple"** by Ashwin Saravanan, a grade 11 student with vision impairment, shares the personal reflections on the temple, appreciating the serenity and introspection it offers while also critiquing the commercialization and crowds.

Ashwin Saravanan also pens a short story titled **"The Ruined House"** about a retired detective who uncovers a smuggling operation being run from a ruined house, showcasing the astute observation and problem-solving skills of an individual who is visually impaired.

A pioneer vision impaired person to excel in manifold facets of life such as technology, profession and personal relationship, B. Kannan reviews the history and challenges of assistive technology for the visually impaired in India, emphasizing the transformative role of Braille, audio materials, computers, and AI-powered tools in enhancing accessibility and inclusion. His article **"State of Visually Impaired in 75 Years of Independent India: Issues and Challenges"** offers a thorough overview of technological progress and its impact in the lives of blind individuals.

In his article titled **"A Forgotten Blind Mathematician Of India"**, Dr. G. S. Ramaiah recounts the remarkable story of Dr. Lakkoju Sanjeevarayalu, a self-taught blind mathematician who achieved extraordinary feats in mathematics despite lacking formal education and facing systemic barriers. Likewise, the article **"Making Of A Specially Abled Doctor"** by Dr. Hitesh Prasad shares the author's personal journey of becoming an Ayurveda physician despite facing progressive vision loss. He discusses the challenges he encountered in his education and career, emphasizing the importance of assistive technologies and supportive communities in enabling him to achieve his goals.

The article **"Towards Financial Inclusion for Persons with Visual Impairment"** presents a much needed discussion for the present scenario. Dr. Sam Taraporevala, Ketan Kothari, and Disha Kapadia-Chinchwadkar explore the barriers faced by visually impaired individuals in accessing financial services in India. They discuss the legal and regulatory mandates for financial inclusion, the ground-level realities of discrimination and inaccessibility, and the way forward to ensure barrier-free access to financial services for persons with visual impairment.

Focusing on the legal dimension, the article **"Journey of Visually Impaired Population in Independent India"** by Mr. Anshul Kapoor and Dr. Biswabhushan Behera examine the statutory provisions for the protection of persons with disabilities in India, focusing on the intersectional identities of visual impairment and the social model of disability. They discuss the challenges faced by visually impaired individuals in accessing education, employment, and other services, advocating for greater inclusion and empowerment.

Raut Nikita and Sameer Latey explore the potential of AI in empowering visually impaired individuals, discussing AI-assisted solutions in education, employment, and independent living in their article **"Navigating the intersection of Visual Impairment & Artificial Intelligence"**. They also address the potential challenges and biases of AI, advocating for inclusive development principles and affordability to ensure equitable access for all.

The article **"Enhancing Spatial Awareness: For the Visually Impaired"** by Pavan Maiya, Pranav Bahven Savla, and Daniel Marc Maani presents the research findings on enhancing spatial awareness for the visually impaired through innovative technologies. The authors discuss the complexities of spatial awareness, existing assistive technologies and their limitations, and the potential of emerging technologies like haptic feedback, AR, and smart environments to revolutionize spatial perception and facilitate independent navigation.

Another experiential essay **"Overcoming Barriers: My Journey as a Student with Visual Impairment in STEM Education"** presents the personal journey of through STEM education the Pranav Bhaven Savla, a software engineering student with visual impairment, highlighting the challenges of inaccessible learning materials and the power of adaptation through assistive technologies and collaborative learning. He discusses the importance of advocacy, support systems, and a resilient mindset in overcoming barriers and achieving success in STEM fields.

The article **"Understanding Individuals With Visual Impairment"** by Sairabanu Daragad and Dr. Venkat Lakshmi provides an overview of visual impairment, discussing its prevalence, categories, identification, causes, features, and challenges faced by visually impaired individuals. The authors emphasize the importance of creating an inclusive environment that accommodates their needs and supports their independence.

Presenting an insider perspective as a non-disabled person, Arasi shares her experiences with visually impaired colleagues and students in the essay **"Champions Of Inner Light!"**, challenging the notion that visual experience is essential for knowledge acquisition and highlighting the unique strengths and communication styles of visually impaired individuals.

All these articles present a rich and varied tapestry of experiences, insights, and perspectives on visual impairment in India. The book thus traverses a broad spectrum of themes, from personal journeys of adaptation and resilience to critical analyses of systemic barriers and advocacy for inclusion.

The personal narratives shared by individuals with visual impairments offer poignant glimpses into the challenges they face in navigating a world not always designed with their needs in mind. These stories illuminate the indomitable human spirit that persists in the face of adversity, showcasing the transformative power of acceptance, determination, and assistive technologies.

The scholarly articles provide in-depth analyses of the social, educational, and economic barriers that hinder the full participation of visually impaired individuals in society. They delve into the concept of intersectionality, recognizing the multiple and intersecting identities that individuals possess and the unique experiences of disability they create. The articles also emphasize the importance of reasonable accommodation, accessible technology, and inclusive policies in empowering visually impaired individuals to achieve their full potential.

This collection thus serves as a valuable resource for students and educators alike, fostering a deeper understanding of disability and society. I earnestly believe that anyone embarking on the journey of learning about disability and society will find this edited volume immensely resourceful, especially for a deeper understanding of blindness and persons with vision impairments. I encourage you to approach these articles with an open mind and a willingness to challenge your preconceived notions about disability. The experiences and perspectives shared in these articles will enrich your understanding of the social model of disability, intersectionality, reasonable accommodation, and the transformative power of assistive technologies. I hope that this collection will inspire blind individuals, disabled persons' organizations, social workers, lawyers, academicians and all other stakeholders to advocate for a more inclusive and equitable society where everyone, regardless of their abilities, has the opportunity to thrive.

Dr. K. Muruganandan,
Assistant Professor and Head,
Department of English,
Government Arts and Science College,
Kallakurichi, Tamil Nadu, India.
Email: *Send2kmn@gmail.com*

Acknowledgment

The outcome of any endeavor is not solely determined by the determination and hard work of an individual but, more importantly, by the collective contributions and unwavering support from the entire ecosystem. At this moment, I would like to take a moment to reflect on the continuous and steadfast support received from a diverse group of people in the creation of this book, '**State of Visually Impaired in 75 Years of Independent India: Issues and Challenges**'.

I am deeply grateful to the trustees of the Karna Vidya Foundation for placing their trust in me and providing the opportunity to shed light on the status of persons with visual impairments in seventy-five years of independent India through this book.

My heartfelt thanks go to Dr. V. Sivaraman, Associate Professor in the Department of English, Presidency College, Chennai, for his invaluable work in reviewing the abstracts and full papers submitted by various authors across India.

I am also deeply appreciative of Dr. Muruganandan, Assistant Professor and Head, Department of English, Government Arts and Science College, Kallakurichi, for his critical and erudite introduction to this book. Without his contribution, this book would not have come to fruition.

I would like to extend my sincere gratitude to each and every author who contributed their knowledge and expertise through their articles. Their wealth of insight and remarkable patience throughout the publication process has been instrumental in bringing this book to life.

A special acknowledgment is due to Mrs. Sarala Ram Kamal, Accessible Content Developer and Trainer, whose selfless dedication was crucial in ensuring that this book achieved a level of quality and accessibility that could reach print-disabled individuals. Her tireless efforts have enabled the creation of this book in an accessible format.

I also wish to express my heartfelt thanks to Notion Press and its team for their dedication and professional efforts in publishing this book in an accessible and effective manner, ensuring it reaches readers across the globe.

Lastly, I would like to extend my gratitude to the activists and friends with visual impairments, whose support and guidance throughout this project have been invaluable in making this book a reality.

Thank you all for your unwavering support and commitment.

Dr. K. Raghuraman,
Assistant Professor, Government Arts College (Autonomous,)
Nandanam, Chennai

Finding Happiness In Sorrows Of Life

Aastha Singhal
Chartered Accountant

I am a late visually impaired person who gradually lost my vision. It feels like I used to live in a completely different world before my vision loss. In that world I was a person who was capable of doing things independently without asking for help. But now the things have changed. Sometimes it feels things are out of my control now. In this world I am learning to accept myself the way I am, to trust and depend upon people around me and also realized that there is no harm in asking for help. There is a feeling within me pushing me to overcome and confront this defeat. But then there are the louder voice creeping in from the shadow of my memories in which I was the heroine of my story.

All those Day-to-day Activities like riding bike, participating in sports, watching movies, travelling all by myself and so on suddenly became privileges which I cannot perform.

But one thing which was clear in my mind was not to give up on my education and complete it in the same way I wanted it to be. So, I continued with my chartered accountancy course.

Back then, I was unaware of screen reading software, scribe facilities, and other accessibility tools, so I persisted with conventional methods. Though I could read, it was at a slow pace. This was the time when my mother, brother and my friends became my support system. My mother and friends would read for me, while my brother provided notes printed in enlarged, high-contrast text. I studied during the daytime and relied on revision videos after sunset, as my ability to read was limited to natural sunlight. On one hand, I needed to concentrate on my exam preparation, while on the other, I was consumed by the stress of whether I'd be able to write for the exam and the unpredictable weather conditions looming over those crucial days.

During that time, I found tremendous inspiration in the words of Martin Luther King Jr:- " If you cant fly then run, if you cant run then walk, if you cant walk then crawl, but whatever you do you have to keep moving forward"

The journey pressed on, and I discovered the option of using a scribe whenever I felt unable to write my exams. The head of my exam center wisely advised against taking unnecessary risks, urging me to apply for a writer as my vision was deteriorating over time.

The time I realized that I need a writer to give my last group of CA final exams was really awful. The thought of not being able to present my knowledge on a piece of paper was a lot to handle, especially just one day before the exam. I was not able to convince myself about the fact that how will I make another person understand the answers I want to present in the exact manner as this was the first time I had to use a writer in my life and that too in such crucial exams like chartered accountancy. My mother gave me the strength to accept the reality and go for it. The outcome took me by surprise as I achieved a score of 92 in one of the subjects. It's a testament to the mysterious ways in which divine intervention may influence our lives... The girl who wrote my exam had such a beautiful handwriting and was so dedicated while writing my exam as it was her own. My family was so proud of me and we all cherished that moment. All the hardships and sorrows took the shape of happiness in that moment.

After completing my CA course, I got connected to visually impaired community, a pivotal moment that reshaped my life's trajectory. They not only offered me invaluable guidance but also enlightened me about accessibility tools that were previously unknown to me. Through their support, I discovered the myriad capabilities of visually impaired individuals, showcasing that despite sight loss, great achievements are possible through alternative pathways. This connection instilled in me a profound sense of belonging and infused the positivity I desperately needed during that phase of my life. By the time I had the realization that by recognizing the positive impacts of our struggles, we become stronger and a better person leaving the bitter behind.

Now, alongside my father and elder brother, I've stepped into our family business. Despite sharing the same disability with my brother, we're both striving to manage it proficiently, pouring our hearts into every aspect. As I reflect on this journey, one profound life lesson stands out: 'Accepting yourself is the beginning of finding happiness you never knew existed.'

How I Approached Maths As A Visually Impaired Student

Abhishek Dhol

Introduction

Maths is a very visual subject, posing some challenges for the blind or partially sighted (visually impaired) student. At the same time, it can be one of the most intellectually rewarding subjects to study at school, as I found. This is largely down to the approaches that were employed to make things accessible for me, an emphasis on sustained and rigorous application and practice and a culture of high expectations that was ingrained in the way things were done to supervise my education by responsible adults.

A. Accessibility

1.   What worked for me

There must always be a focus on producing materials for the visually impaired student in a way that will get them to understand concepts at the same level of depth as would be the case for a sighted student. The reality of the education systems in most countries is that students will be required to undertake public (externally set and assessed) examinations to progress from one stage of their schooling to another, or to earn the qualification(s) that will permit them to leave school and move to higher education or employment. Therefore, clarity on exam boards' reasonable adjustments policies for visually impaired students is absolutely vital, in order to ensure that students can do justice to themselves in these examinations, especially any that are taken on or after the age of sixteen, which tend to have impacts on students' admission to universities. This was what was done for me. The exams officers for my school for the Cambridge and IB exam boards communicated to me, my family and my teachers what adjustments were permitted and how they would be implemented, and, as far as was possible in the Indian context, these approaches were used. For example, the Cambridge system has a public examination taken by students in the 8th grade called the Checkpoint. This effectively acts as a 'practice board exam'. In this, we understood that I would be supplied with raised diagrams with Braille labels on PIAF printers (so-called 'Minolta Diagrams') by the exam board. A printer similar to the one used was purchased and used to create all diagrams relating to my school's internal tests and examinations, in preparation for what I would face in the external ones. In addition, CAIE and IB consider it to be good practice to allow a teacher familiar with the subject in question with whom the student has practiced before to be an amanuensis or reader. This was done in my case. A paraprofessional educator who worked in my school's department for disabled and neurodiverse students provided tactile and verbal explanations for what was being taught/demonstrated in class, while also acting as a scribe for me. In comparison, I find the approaches used by some domestic exam boards (of getting a younger student/ student in a lower stage of education to be a reader/scribe) to be disappointing. It must be remembered that while any adjustment must not put a disabled student at an advantage, it must not have the reverse effect either. As Maths has a specific lexicon and as a Maths teacher would be best able to pronounce/read this terminology or verbalize/describe visual diagrams/aspects of diagrams to a student, I don't see why this arrangement couldn't be implemented for other students as well, with appropriate guardrails being in place (e.g., ensuring the teacher is also not the invigilator). The current arrangement, unfortunately, could result in a student being put at a disadvantage.

2.   Aspects for further consideration

There are two key things that were not thought out very well by my exam board.

First, the tactile versions of shapes in questions about prism volumes etc. were presented in two-dimensional format. Understanding diagrams presented like this requires a level of visualisation that is often exceedingly difficult for visually impaired students. Arranging three-dimensional alternatives would be a meaningful change to present practices.

Secondly, in my 10th grade Cambridge board exams, the rules allowed for the assistance I received with adaptive equipment to be only limited in scope (e.g., requiring me to hold a scale while drawing a line). While it is useful to get students to practice these things, the focus on getting visually impaired students to spend time and effort drawing and manipulating equipment (as opposed to doing perhaps some manipulation of equipment and, based on their understanding, instructing/asking for assistance) is a tendency to emphasize on a shallow version of craft, rather than on demonstrating a strong conceptual understanding. Therefore, keeping in mind the disproportionate effort visually impaired students must put in because these tasks are more challenging for them, widening the scope for scribes to assist with drawing tasks would help make things more accessible.

B.   Sustained application and practice

It must be acknowledged that even for the brightest visually impaired student, the process of understanding most visual concepts is likely to be more time-consuming. The curriculum of most exam boards, in their current form—designed for sighted students—will require the average visually impaired student to put in twice the amount of effort to understand what their sighted counterparts take to understand. It was my custom from the 9th grade onwards to practice Maths questions from textbooks and previous years' exams every day of the week for several hours. An old exam paper that took my sighted counterparts two hours to solve took me over three, with all the drawing, showing of detailed working and graph plotting I had to do. At the same time, I knew that rushing things could result in silly mistakes. Therefore, going into this with open eyes and a willingness and understanding that applying oneself thoroughly is the only recipe to success I can suggest.

C.   Culture of high expectations

At school, I often felt that in one way, my counterparts taking Indian exam boards were luckier than me—they had to deal with lowered expectations in terms of content difficulty, as my understanding is that many exam boards allow for diagrammatic questions to be replaced with non-visual alternatives. I am, however, now of the opinion that this is a bonfire of academic standards. As there are methods to make things accessible, this (replacing visual questions with alternatives) is no longer a proportionate means of achieving a legitimate aim (levelling the playing field). While I have described another method of levelling the playing field above (widening the rules around assistance with drawing tasks), the other great equaliser is ensuring everyone has the same knowledge and is evaluated on the same content. By ensuring I learned and was evaluated on everything my sighted counterparts learned and were evaluated on, the education system I went through held me to as rigorous a standard as anyone else, even if it failed to level the playing field in terms of effort levels to be successful.

Conclusion

Maths, if learned and taught well, can be a foundation for a successful career. As a challenging subject, strong performance in it is regarded (with justification) by universities and employers as a reliable indicator of intellectual ability. I am of the opinion that enhancing and building on the approach that worked for me could open up a plethora of opportunities for visually impaired people, leading to their long-term empowerment.

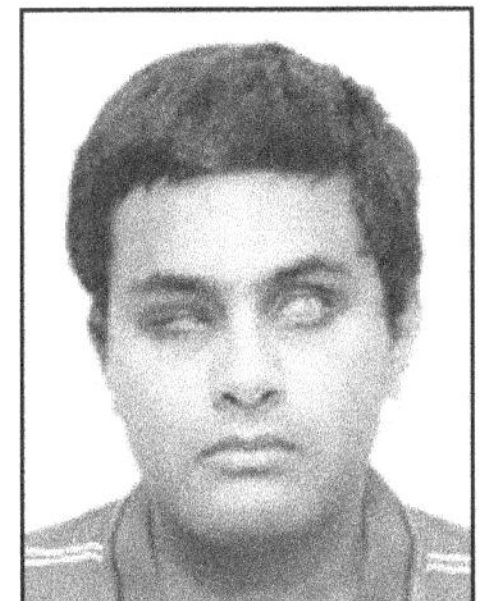

Abhishek Dhol *is born in New Delhi, India, in 2003. He grew up in Bangalore and attended Bangalore International School, a Cambridge school and an IB World School.*

He studied Maths, Physics and Chemistry until the 12th grade. He was clear that he wanted to be a lawyer from a young age, he did Maths and Science subjects partially because these are requirements for the exam board qualifications he was registered for and because these are considered to be essential study for admission in many of the world's best universities located in the global north (admissions for some undergraduate programmes at such institutions clearly list these subjects as de jure requirements, while there is sufficient empirical evidence to indicate that even for the purposes of subjects like Law, Maths is treated in these places as a de facto requirement). He also felt (correctly as it turned out) that studying a mixture of approaches to problem solving (the analytical/normative/argumentative approach of History, English or Economics and also the empirical, step-by-step approach of Maths and Science) would be a strong foundation for the law studies.

After completing the schooling, he immigrated to the United Kingdom (UK) to study law at the undergraduate level. Abhishek completed the Bachelor of Laws (LLB) at Queen Mary in July 2024, and returned there for the Master of Laws (LLM) in September this year.

Abhishek's eye condition is called Retinopathy of Prematurity (RoP). He didn't have any sight since the age of four.

Gender And Disability

Ambika Khattar
PhD scholar: 2023-2024

Abstract:

In this paper, I aim to provide concise definitions of disability and gender, examine the similarities and differences between the two terms, explore the reasons behind the high dropout rates of girls from schools, discuss the historical denial of admission to inclusive schools for girls before the 21st century, and shed light on how their disabled and non-disabled male counterparts subject them to acts of sexual violence.

I chose this topic because, as a visually impaired girl, I can personally relate to the challenges faced by women with disabilities. These women have been a source of inspiration for me, showcasing resilience in the face of adversity.

Keywords:

Disability, Gender, Visual Impairment, Inclusive Education, Emotional rape, sexual violence, and discrimination.

I would like to share the struggles my parents and I encountered while searching for a school after I learned Braille from the National Association for the Blind in Delhi. Principals and teachers from various schools repeatedly asserted that I would not be able to study in an inclusive school due to the difference in the medium of study. They claimed that it would be challenging to teach me alongside sighted children. I express my heartfelt thanks to my parents, my sister Mehak, and my teacher, Ms. Shweta Thakur, as they played a crucial role in shaping who I am today.

According to the Persons with Disabilities (Equal Opportunities, Protection of Rights and Full Participation) Act, 1995, a "person with a disability" is someone suffering from not less than forty percent of any disability as certified by a medical authority specified for the purposes of this Act by notification from the appropriate Government. The act defines "disability" to include (i) blindness, (ii) low vision, (iii) leprosy-cured, (iv) hearing impairment, (v) locomotor disability, (vi) mental retardation, and (vii) mental illness.

Although gender and disability are linked, I think they slightly differ from each other. The image of disability may be intensified by gender - for women, a sense of intensified passivity and helplessness; for men, a corrupted masculinity generated by enforced dependence. Moreover, these images have real consequences in terms of education, employment, living arrangements, and personal relationships, victimization, and abuse that then reinforce the images in the public sphere. The gendered experience of disability reveals sustained patterns of difference between men and women. For people with disabilities, gendering is conditional onset, which is combined with the type of impairment leading to gender expectations.

Women and girls with disabilities have been invisible, both to advocates of women's rights and of disability rights. In other words, women with disabilities are still not counted even in the marginalized section of Indian society, and this has increased their vulnerability. According to M.S. Abha Kheterpal, women with disabilities face triple discrimination in today's society because they are more prone to physical abuse by their friends and family members. As a result, women with disabilities often must confront additional disadvantages even in comparison to men with disabilities and women without disabilities. I am on the same page with Abha mam because discrimination with disabled girls takes place in special schools too. When I was studying at NAB Delhi, one of my non-disabled teachers always used to remark that I am visually as well as mentally disabled, and she wanted to put me in MHU. According to her, I was a multi-disabled child.

There is a deep relationship between gender and disability, as many girls leave their schools due to poor sanitation facilities, self-esteem issues, the confidence gap, and verbal and physical abuse in classrooms. Limited family support and financial resources exacerbate these challenges.

However, there are some statistics related to the intersectionality of gender and disability, as follows:

- The 2011 World Report on Disability indicates that the female disability prevalence rate is 19.2%, whereas it is 12% for men.

- The global literacy rate is as low as 3% for all adults with disabilities and 1% for women with disabilities.

- Women and girls with disabilities experience higher rates of gender-based violence, sexual abuse, neglect, maltreatment, and exploitation than women and girls without disabilities.

Various commissions took steps to uplift the condition of women as well as handicapped children in India during the colonial and post-colonial era. The Secondary Education Commission of 1952 recommended that women should be educated at par with men. Two divergent views are presented regarding women's education. The first view holds that the home is the only place meant for women, and they need to be educated differently from boys. Any professional training should not be imparted to them. The second view states that women are an eminent part of the public; hence, education is a must for their survival, and they should be taught the same syllabus as men. Home Science was recommended to be taught to both girls and boys. Co-education at the Primary and University levels was encouraged, but there was a need felt to have separate schools for girls and boys at the secondary level as they advanced to the stage of adolescence. On the other hand, if separate schools are created for girls, many of them would remain uneducated due to the orthodox attitude and the financial dependence of their families. They should be provided with at least one woman teacher and separate sanitary conveniences, retiring rooms, playing fields, etc., for their well-being. Girls should get an equal chance to participate in activities like Girls Guiding, Home Nursing, Needlework, etc.

The National Policy on Education 1986 (Ministry of Human Resource Development) also focuses on access to quality education for all students. It proposed the provision of equal opportunities for everyone. Women's education should be facilitated, and they should be imparted technical, professional, and vocational education. Moreover, it also suggested that handicapped children must have feasible access to education, and special schools with residential facilities must be set up. It gave emphasis on inclusiveness for the handicapped in all schools, be it public schools, residential schools, or government-owned schools. The National

Policy of Education (NPE), 1986, and the Programme of Action (POA), 1992, act as the guiding force influencing both the qualitative and quantitative indicators regarding the need for the empowerment of women. The NPE and POA laid stress on the problems of universalization of elementary education as, in essence, the problem of the girl child. They stressed on the increasing participation of girls at all stages of education, particularly in streams like sciences, vocational, technical, and commerce education. The POA also stressed the need for reorienting the education system to promote women's equality in education.

Life is a struggle for women and girls with disabilities in India. It is a harsh reality that they encounter more cases of sexual violence, referring to the act of forcing a girl to have sex or engage in sexual activities without her consent. There is no data available on the sexual violence faced by women and girls with disabilities in India. According to Shampa Sengupta, the same kind of treatment should be given to women and girls with disabilities as is given to other non-disabled women and girls. She reported that not a single mainstream protest has been organized to protect their rights. According to a 2018 report by Human Rights, women and girls with disabilities face significant barriers to justice and a higher risk of sexual violence. Rape is a type of sexual assault involving sexual intercourse or other forms of sexual penetration carried out against a person without their consent. Abha Kheterpal, in her book "Disabled Lives Matter," talks about a term called "Emotional Rape," which she defines as the "defilement of emotions, feelings, and, above all, the human soul." Marriage is a distant dream for girls with disabilities. According to M.S. Abha Kheterpal, "In such a culture that overwhelmingly values youth and beauty, women with disabilities are found at the lowest level of the totem pole of love and romance." I think that people are only concerned with the physical beauty of a woman; that is why they demean a disabled woman and seek a perfect girl who can handle household responsibilities. People have forgotten the concept of inner beauty nowadays. That's why the rate of loneliness is higher among girls with disabilities compared to their non-disabled peers.

To conclude, I think that these things can be overcome by making those girls understand their rights, providing them with immediate medical care if sexual violence happens, and conducting government workshops for free for such girls. The government should also set up a special phone line for women and girls to call if sexual violence happens to them, opening new avenues for the brighter future of girls and women with disabilities.

List of books and articles on gender and Disability:

1. "Disabled Women, an Excluded Agenda of Indian Feminism" by Anita Ghai (2006)

2. "Women, Disability, and Identity" by Asha Hans and Annie Patri (2003)

3. "Invisible Victims of Sexuality Violence: Access to Justice for Disabled Women in India" by Nidhi Goyal (2018)

4. "Disabled Lives Matter" by Abha Kheterpal (2022).

Ambika Khattar
Email: - *ambikakhattar2@gmail.com*

Journey of Visually Impaired Population in Independent India - Challenges & way forward

Mr. Anshul Kapoor & Dr. Biswabhushan Behera

Abstract:

A disability is a condition that impairs a person's ability to perform tasks, participate in daily activities, or interact with others on a developmental, mental, physical, or cognitive level. It's a word used to characterise a disability or a long-term health issue that keeps someone from working for pay. ICMR data from the 2019–2021 NHFS survey indicates that 63.28 million people, or 4.52% of the population, are estimated to be disabled overall. Over 23% of the population in India has some form of Visually Handicap situation, and 1.2 billion youngsters there currently suffer from eye-related illnesses. There has been little progress made towards the aim of granting the disabled equal rights and advantages, despite the voices of those who supported it demanding it. The effort gained much-needed momentum in 1995 when the Indian government passed the PWD Act in response to multiple protests and agitations. Reservations were granted for up to 3% of all jobs in government and educational organizations. This was never enough, though, as the disabled community remained marginalised and their requests to move from one pillar to another were unmet. The phenomenon transcends cultural, political, and geographic barriers to understanding the distinct behaviours exhibited as well as the ways and times in which even members of homogeneous groups behave differently in different settings. By examining the various statutory enactments in India for the protection of PWDs, the intersectional identities of visual impairment, intersectionality, and the social model of disability, as well as the exemptions from the law known as "reasonable accommodations" for accommodating these underrepresented groups in society, the article seeks to understand the issues surrounding visually handicapped people and identify the various challenges they face.

Keywords: Disability, PWD, Visually Impaired, reasonable accommodations

Introduction:

Disability is the term used to describe an impairment or a persistent medical condition that precludes a person from engaging in gainful employment. A disability is defined as a reduction in capacity, disqualification, or disadvantage in a particular circumstance or while carrying out a task. Finally, a disadvantage in an individual's incapacity relative to others is referred to as a disability. Disability is a compound word that combines the words "disadvantage" and "ability," denoting that when a person's ability is impaired due to circumstances outside of their control, they are labelled as having special needs and are accordingly stereotyped.

When the phrase was first used in 1574, it meant that a person could be regarded as external and to have a privative, negative, or reversing force. The term "handicapped" came from a barter betting game with a hand and a cap that was played in the United Kingdom in 1653. From 1915 until 1958, the term "handicapped" was used to refer to children who were handicapped. After that, it was widely used to refer to all forms of disabilities in society.

Objectives:

This article aims to examine the several statutory enactments in India that protect people with disabilities and gain an understanding of the intersectional identities of visual impairment, intersectionality, disability social model, reasonable accommodations and comprehend the concerns & challenges faced by Visually impaired.

Research Methodology:

This paper's study is based on exploratory library research using secondary data and information from relevant books, journals, periodicals, articles, media reports, and other online sources. The research design of the study is descriptive; it has been thoroughly analyzed; and it has made full use of secondary data that are readily available.

Literature Review:

Twenty percent of the world's visually handicapped people live in India. Given the significant proportion of this community compared to the rest of the disabled, the government has worked to integrate this group into society ever since independence. The Indian government has implemented a number of programmes for people with vision impairments in the areas of employment, education, and other areas for this reason. Even with the development of numerous such programmes, the true challenge remained in making these well-established programmes accessible to the appropriate target population (Venkatesan & Udhayakumar, 2015).

A person's entire life is hampered by blindness, but education is particularly detrimental because it is unquestionably the foundation of a nation's progress and development. It obviously should be concerning for a nation that works hard to become a developed nation (Tripathi, 2018).

People with visual impairment can perform a wide range of jobs and can be dependable workers, if they are accommodated suitably for their loss of vitals, which are essentially needed on their jobs (Dong, Guerette, Warner, Zalles, & Mamboleo, 2017).

India has made great progress in eradicating preventable blindness. Since the last national survey, the prevalence of blindness and visual impairment has decreased dramatically. To properly address the issue, a thorough and committed approach is necessary, as the problem still presents a considerable hurdle to achieving universal eye health. Focus is especially needed to enhance the nation's cataract surgery procedures, corneal transplantation, and eye banking services, as well as to successfully incorporate refractive treatments into the current eye care system (Vashist, et al., 2022).

Psychosocial disorders such as depression, social isolation, cognitive decline, increasing reliance on others, and low self-rated health are linked to visual impairment. Poorer visual function has been linked to limitations in daily living activities, physical performance, and mobility. Moving from one place to another without help is one of the biggest obstacles. Other difficulties include having trouble identifying individuals and spotting obstructions. Children's development is supported from an early age by orientation, mobility, and independence training, which enables blind and partially sighted children to participate actively in the family, school, and social settings alongside their sighted classmates (Edward, Edward, & V, 2022).

Disability in India:

According to data provided by ICMR from the NHFS survey 2019–2021, the overall percentage of the population with disabilities is 4.52%, or 63.28 million people. The number of disabled people increased from 21 million in the 2001 census to 26.8 million in the 2011 census. India signed and ratified the United Nations Convention on the Rights of Persons with Disabilities on March 30, 2007, making it a party to the convention. The National Trust Act of 1999, the Mental Healthcare Act of 2017, the Rights of Persons with Disability Act of 2016, and the Rehabilitation Council of India Act of 1992 are the several laws about disability. India passed the Full Participation Act of 1995 as well as the Equal Opportunity Protection of Rights for Persons with Disabilities. The RPWD Act of 2016 raised the reservation percentage in all government occupations and educational institutions from 3% to 4% and included 21 different categories of disabilities in its scope. Currently, 1.2 billion children in India suffer from diseases related to their eyes, and over 23% of the country's population has some sort of eye problem.

Disability after independence:

Prioritising the development of the Indian economy was crucial while it was just emerging from the constraints of oppressive British control. To combat poverty and achieve self-sufficiency in the production of food grains, five-year plans focused heavily on economic growth and development. As agriculture was the only source of income for about 70% of Indians, industry and foreign trade were still in their infancy. Policies were developed against this backdrop for the less fortunate segments of society, including the scheduled castes, tribes, and OBCs. However, regrettably, the disabled, who made up the remaining portion of the Indian labour force, were ignored and had no say in questions of policy.

Although some voices were calling for the disabled to have equal rights and privileges, there was little movement towards that goal. For the welfare of the disabled and to further their cause, a large number of NGOs grew during the 1980s. Following several demonstrations and agitations, the Indian government enacted the The PWD (Equal Opportunities, Protection of Rights, and Full Participations) Act, 1995, providing the campaign with much-needed momentum. Up to 3% of all positions in government employment and educational institutions were reserved for reservations. However, this was never sufficient because the disabled people continued to be a disenfranchised community, their desires to shift from one pillar to another unheeded.

The conversation around disabilities changed with the adoption of the Convention on the Rights of Persons with Disabilities (CRPD). In 2007, India reaffirmed its commitment to protecting the rights of people with disabilities by signing and ratifying the UNCRPD. Although the 1995 disability Act was a welfare-based policy, it did not address the differences between the needs of the disabled and the resources that were available. The recognition of PWDs as subjects with rights as opposed to objects was made possible in large part by this Act.

Unfortunately, there are still strong institutional, cultural, and physical obstacles separating the disabled from the general population. In contrast to their able-bodied peers, 15% of the world's population, according to the World Bank, has a disability and suffers socio-economic obstacles. The RPWD Act of 2016 superseded the earlier 1995 Act, which was in line with the UNCRPD's principles. The 2016 Act forbids discrimination, allows for reasonable accommodations, enforces inclusive education, guarantees equal opportunities with accessibility in educational institutions, and encourages inclusive policies and practices. In addition to offering accessible and reasonably priced healthcare facilities, specialised care and rehabilitation services, barrier-free access to accessible infrastructure, accessible transportation, public transportation, and assistive devices to improve mobility and ensure independent travel, it also encourages the creation of barrier-free work environments.

Inter-sectional identities of visual impairment:

Cultural, political, and geographic barriers are transcended under the phenomena in order to comprehend the various behaviours displayed as well as how and when even members of homogeneous groups behave differently in various contexts. An approach called intersectionality aims to explain how many communities' experiences are shaped by the combination and shifting of social structures and institutions such as the state, its educational system, and government programmes, as well as conditions such as being a woman or disabled. A concept known as intersectionality can be used to better explain why people differ in their experiences with and preferences for common characteristics such as gender, race, age, disability, ethnicity, sexual orientation, and gender identity. The intersectionality method assumes that a person's experiences and decisions vary depending on the intricate interplay between their interpersonal and group relationships.

Reading content in braille instead of relying on someone else would undoubtedly change how a blind person feels and create an entirely new experience because the person reading the material in braille will likely have preconceived notions about the subject. In addition to improving comprehension and raising questions, self-reading fosters stakeholder involvement and establishes the groundwork for ultimately succeeding in independently obtaining services. The disabled can dispel societal preconceptions about their capacity for autonomous thought, action, and decision-making by successfully obtaining all service components. A disabled person gains self-sufficiency and independence through this type of exposure. The inability of the disabled to travel independently and avoid being a laughingstock for others makes it difficult for them to receive unwelcome assistance. The availability of appliances and aids makes a person feel on par with their able-bodied counterparts.

Intersectionality and the social model of disability:

A person's physical environment, attitudes, public policies, and socially constructed experiences all contribute to their disability. Disadvantageous circumstances can make a person impaired and make it more difficult for them to be accepted by society. Although able-bodied people rarely think of an office block with stairs as a barrier, wheelchair users frequently find them to be so. Because men and women have distinct requirements in the same situations, intersectionality helps us grasp the unique experiences that these two groups have. For the same mobility objective, two disabled people might use a wheelchair and a cane, for instance.

Using a cane to enter a place inaccessible by wheelchair is possible, although it can occasionally be dangerous due to uneven terrain. Here, the facilitation is contingent upon the decisions made and the ensuing consequences of the circumstances. When a disabled person relies on public transportation with varying routes and stops, the situation can get worse. A person with disabilities may find it difficult to discern the bus's itinerary and may become discouraged about reaching his destination. The social model highlights the hurdles that PWDs face in society, and intersectionality enables us to comprehend how the elements that make up a decision in a particular scenario influence our preferences and choices.

The 2011 census indicates that PWDs report lower income levels than the abled, with the biggest disparity being during employable years. It was determined that service providers and staff needed immediate training on the necessities for providing services to the visually impaired, as well as disability-related training. The visually impaired expressed their frustration at not being able to find a reasonably priced property close to public transit and their wish to have educational and medical amenities nearby within their budget. It is accurate to claim that experiences, preferences, and reality are far removed from public policy; visually impaired people discovered that the most economical home was also the most inaccessible.

Reasonable accommodation:

Exemptions from the law known as "reasonable accommodations" are added to make it more accommodating to underrepresented groups in society. It is the responsibility of every employer to offer equitable and just working conditions, as well as reasonable accommodations that enable all job seekers and workers to have equal opportunity for employment and career advancement. A reasonable accommodation is defined as a setting in which each employee is at ease and has all of his requirements met so that he can work. Granting equitable accommodations to all workers not only boosts output but also cultivates a devoted and innovative workforce and readies the company for unfavourable circumstances. Additionally, making a fair concession helps the employee feel more confident and prepared for their job.

The Honourable Supreme Court of India states that reasonable accommodations for people with disabilities have the following roles and values:

1. A duty on the part of the government and private sector to give people with disabilities (PWDs) extra assistance and facilities so they can participate in society.

2. The right to equality and nondiscrimination guaranteed by the constitution is a guarantee to people with disabilities (PWDs) through reasonable accommodation.

3. The executive branch must take a liberal stance when it comes to providing help to people with disabilities; it cannot be obstinate or inert.

4. To address disability, it is necessary to actively create environments that support the growth of individuals with disabilities.

5. Accommodations must be customised to meet the specific needs of each impairment.

Students can respond to their surroundings, synthesise information, and learn by accident thanks to their sense of vision. Through the provision of information and stimulus, vision channels movement. It also integrates and organises information in the brain to facilitate social interactions. We are only drawn to other people, things, environments, and beauty through our vision. Any loss of eyesight leaves one vulnerable to assumptions about their surroundings, forcing them to rely on their other senses to make sense of their immediate circumstances. While there are various appliances and aids available to provide some comfort to those whose vision cannot be corrected with lenses, replacing one's eyes is nearly impossible.

Accommodations might alter based on each person's demands, which means they are customised with preference. However, the following are provided to ensure their comfortable working environment:

1. Adjustments that are required like large typefaces, colour contrasts, and scribes for exams.

2. Assistive devices like braille embossers, screen reading software, magnifiers, etc.

3. Modified course materials

4. Task guidelines in an accessible manner

5. Adaptable work hours including Work from home

6. Regular vacation time

7. Company-paid pick-up and drop

8. Directional wall and floor changes, accessible elevators, and restrooms.

9. Labelling electrical switches, exit routes, doors, and staircases

10. Reorganisation or editing of the job description.

Conclusion:

It is imperative that an inclusive education strategy be put into place in all Indian schools and across the board. Children with vision impairments must eventually be enrolled in regular middle or high schools and not in special schools. To ensure that blind students lead very healthy and pleasant lives, the government should build more rehabilitation facilities, give them excellent training, give them preference when it comes to work chances, and hire psychologists. In general, the blind are forced to fall behind in society, so they have a long way to go before they can successfully integrate. Attitude and social barriers impact programmes at every level. The blind on a continuum will be empowered by sustained efforts and candid conversations for better support services, reducing their demand for social programmes over time. The appropriate actions and measures needs to be taken by altering current statutory laws and bye-laws in order to bring visually handicapped people into social inclusion.

References

Cai, C., Cui, F., & Chang, X. (2024). Consciousness Awakening and Technology Enabling - A Case Study of Self-Supporting of Persons with Visual Impairments in Inclusive Higher Education. Review of Disability Studies: An International Journal, 19(1), 1-43.

Dong, S., Guerette, A., Warner, A., Zalles, M. Z., & Mamboleo, G. (2017). Barriers in Accommodation Process Among Individuals with Visual Impairments. Journal of Rehabilitation, 83(2), 27-35.

Dong, S., Mullins, M., & Ostrowicz, I. (2021). Factors influencing workplace accommodations requests among employees with visual impairments. The Australian Journal of Rehabilitation Counselling, 27, 90–101.

Edward, S., Edward, V., & V, K. (2022). Level of Independence and the Mental Status of the Visually Challenged High School Students in Chennai. National Journal of Community Medicine, 13(2), 100-103. doi: 10.55489/njcm1322022158

Iyundhu, A., Karooma, C., & Emong, P. (2021). Complying with Reasonable Accommodation Requirements for Persons with Visual Impairment in Uganda Public Service Employment? Assumptions and Gaps. Advances in Social Sciences Research Journal, 8(3), 632–651. doi:https://doi.org/10.14738/assrj.83.9877

Jadhav, S. V., & Jagdeo, K. R. (2020). Right of Accessibility of Visually Impaired under Indian Copyright Law-A Critical Study. International Journal of Creative Research Thoughts (IJCRT), 8(6), 983-990.

Matsuzaki, Y., Hamamatsu, W., & Shibata, K. (1-15). Difficulties in the workplace for people with borderline personality disorder: A literature review. Pacific Rim International Conference on Disability and Diversity Conference Proceedings (p. 2020). Honolulu, Hawai'i: Center on Disability Studies, University of Hawai'i at Mānoa.

O'Donnell, W. (2014). An Analysis of Employment Barriers Facing Blind People. University of Massachusetts Boston.

Tripathi, P. V. (2018). Educating visually imparied in India. Journal of Emerging Technologies and Innovative Research (JETIR), 5(3), 1313-1315.

Vashist, P., Senjam, S. S., Gupta, V., Gupta, N., Shamann, B. R., Wadhwani, M., . . . Bharadwaj, A. (2022). Blindness and visual impairment and their causes in India: Results of a nationally representative survey. PLOS ONE, 17(7), 1-14.

Venkatesan, P., & Udhayakumar, S. (2015). A study on utilization of specific Government Schemes among the visually challenged students of selected colleges in Coimbatore, Coimbatore District. Indian Journal of Applied Research, 5(12), 124-126.

Mr. Anshul Kapoor, *M.B.A., PGDPM, NET.*

Sr. Superintendent (HR), GAIL (India) Limited,

Email: anshulkapoor1979@gmail.com

A HR Professional with more than 18 years of rich experience in Human Resource Management with India's No.1 Gas Transmission & Distribution Company and youngest Maharatna Company. Currently designated as Sr. Superintendent (HR) with GAIL (India) Limited and responsible for Employees' Services, PF, Pension & Superannuation and Post-Retirement Medical Scheme at GAIL, Corporate Office, New Delhi.

A Management Graduate with M.B.A. (HR) from Annamalai University, Tamil Nadu and PGDPM from YMCA, New Delhi.

Published 3 Research Papers at National and International Level.

Dr. Biswabhushan Behera, *Ph.D. (Management), M.B.A., LL.B., NET.*

Dy. General Manager (HR), GAIL (India) Limited,

Email: bbb222@rediffmail.com

A senior HR Professional with more than 22 years of rich experience in Human Resource Management with India's No.1 Gas Transmission & Distribution Company and youngest Maharatna Company. Currently designated as Deputy General Manager (HR) with GAIL (India) Limited, Corporate Office, New Delhi, and handling Corporate HR Policy, Employee Relations, Labour Law Compliances & Contract Management at GAIL Corporate Office.

A Management Graduate with M.B.A. (HR & Systems) from Utkal University, Bhubaneswar, Odisha, a Law Graduate with LL.B. from Rajasthan University, Jaipur, Rajasthan and Ph.D. from Galgotias University, Greater Noida, Uttar Pradesh. Attended MDPs from IIM- Kolkata, IIM-Lucknow, IMI-Delhi, ISB-Hyderabad and EDPLLM from XLRI, Jamshedpur.

Published 15 Research Papers at National and International Level.

A Life Member of NIPM and nominated as Hony. Additional Secretary of NIPM Delhi NCR Chapter.

Champions Of Inner Light!

S. Arasi

HOD PG and research department of English, Pachaiyappa's College, Chennai 30

Abstract

A few days ago I happened to be talking to my colleague at my college and was stunned by the knowledge he had in any field of thought; although the God Almighty had deprived him the power of sight.

This made me reminisce about the people who are visually impaired and who have succeeded in their life and emerged as a phoenix from their deprived state to accomplishment. My first astonishment was at the Academic Staff College – Orientation Programme where my friend and colleague and I happened to be in the class with Dr. V. Sivaraman.

It was a casual day until the Resource Person for the second session was on; the teacher was dwelling upon the topic on a teacher's life and the methodologies of teaching, while explaining a certain point in teaching methods regarding LISTENING he reeled out a definition that was quite long and winding. And he had the peculiar method of making us LISTEN first; then start jotting down the points and references. Since the definition was quite long and many of us wanted him to repeat it. He plainly refused and challenged whether anyone of us can try repeating what he had uttered "word by word" – the entire class fell into a pin drop silence. When a hand confidently shot up from the front row saying "Shall I?" It was none other than our classmate Dr. V. Sivaraman the entire class was looking at him with admiration as he started to retell the definition "verbatim", the teacher applauded his astounding sense of understanding and recollecting talent. It was predicted that he would reach great heights. And now the attribute which I intentionally left out in this narration is that Dr. Sivaraman was visually impaired but differently gifted. Now my study dwells upon the topic of gifts that are showered on people who are deprived of, one of the main sense of seeing. Let us analyse.

Key words:

Life, Visual Impairment, Deprived or Gifted, Positivity or drudgery – Literary reference.

Champions Of Inner Light!

Let's trace the development of sight of a human with a close study of a baby which at birth can recognise only black and white (a little of grey); which then slowly gains the power of tracking movements followed by basic colours and a binocular vision only in the end of its fourth month. Till then it's a blurred vision and moving object recognition and correcting its own wandering eyes, muscle growth and strengthening are the few stages the baby undergoes progressive vision clarity. Babies learn to use their vision successfully only when their body moves (i.e.) which is not until they are twelve months old.

As the baby grows visual dominance becomes strikingly stronger and disguises the importance of other senses. Whereas a visually impaired child has to completely depend upon, only "ON OTHER FOUR SENSES." Taking a break, now the focus is on the environment in which a growing visually challenged individual and ask the question "Is the world ready and safe for a person deprived of sight?" "Is it filled with sensitised sapiens who can understand the difficulties of the visually impaired?"

Though the paper tries to trace the rosy side of the life led by the visually impaired among the world that is filled with mysteries of its own, remaining unexplored by the people who have visual dominance it also tries to pick up the trail not so long thought to have existed. Hence it simultaneously, explores the challenges the visually impaired face in their day to day life. In order to understand that the five basic senses that are often considered as individual systems that cover visual, auditory, taste, smell, orientation and sensations, there is inter-relations between the senses. The summation of these five senses results in the quality we call, PERCEPTION. These biological tools equip the mind and enable the individual to experience the environment through the five senses, normally. Let us try to analyse the usage of words as I trace back in my experience with VI (visually Impaired) colleagues and students as their perception of the environment, which may be used to identify the common grounds they share. A very interesting anecdote needs to be shared when I happened to accompany a VI person and the normal architect to a Floor Tile showroom; the architect and the client were selecting floor tiles for the stairs. A cute metaphor rolled out to describe the stairs as "stairs being the spine of the house" and exhibited the VI person's subjective use of language with the level of 'semantic specificity' and the conversation on the whole had very little repetition of words or utterances. The vocabulary and metaphor used give meanings that are more experiential with more attention to other senses than sight. In other words visually impaired people use verbalism correctly from a syntactic and semantic point of view.

Yet another, incident at the work place, a newly appointed faculty of English Mr. Vikas Munot entered the department, it was made sure that he had a seat that would make him comfortable. He was the only visually impaired person in the department. Hence all the faculty members wanted to know the answer for a whole bunch of questions that had so long remained unanswered. He was the crux of the department to let the sighted people into his forte' so the unanswered questions were answered. Vikas exhibited grand vocabulary and flair in his accents by which it was comprehensible that his accent was acquired through auditory senses. This negates the view that Bertrand Russell supported along with the great philosophers who declared that knowledge is derived from experience. And he also argued that there is a kind of knowledge that cannot be coded into language. This knowledge is sensory and "direct"(knowledge by acquaintance), connected to the sensory system, and is the basis of the construction of a physical world. With this theory, a visually impaired person being deprived of this important component of experience, namely the vision, comprehends the world in a different way from those who have no visual impairment. Consequently, the conceptual system may be considered defective. This theory of the philosophers is yet to be substantiated, as the antithesis prevails that mastery of language becomes the mediator for the sighted individuals and visually impaired. Language is seen as a tool for understanding the world around us (knowledge by description).

This, then means as two conflicting theories exist in philosophy, psychology too has two divergent theories. Piaget (1964) suggested that language plays a secondary role in the development of knowledge (thought precedes language), whereas Vygotsky (1985) advocates that language has a crucial place in cognitive development (language is seen as a tool for planning and controlling mental activity). So where does the difficulty for the visually impaired lies? It lies in the practical day to day chores which are to be calculated measures as falsely depicted in the popular movies and media. We see the protagonist using echo-location to shoot his targets. This theory of using language through description cannot be generalised for all visually impaired people.

Desamma, my first jubilant, cheerful student who joined literature class and as she stepped into the class and introduced herself, the class and me knew here is someone special. She had a loud and clear voice, a slim stature, neat dressing sense (of course the mother had taken care of her grooming) but she was born with visual impairment. She was a good listener and was adept in taking notes in Braille, the notes that were usually dictated. Had she been alive she would have been an excellent motivator for many a person who though were gifted with vision but did not know how to use it and take care of it. Her reason for leaving this world was the viral fever which made her weak from which she couldn't recover. Medicines led her to depression and slowly leading her to the inevitable death before she could finish her graduation. The language she knew and her skills in debates and oratory were of no use to lift her up from the deep depression. Her dependency on her elderly mother was so deep that she was not able to cope with when her mother fell sick. Her knowledge which she had acquired through description did not give her the hope she had to survive and then shine in this world.

Dr. Kaarkuzhali working in our sister concern Chellammal College for Women is yet another achiever though she mastered her way to become an economically empowered woman, heart of heart I do know her pain that she had gone through in this materialistic world. She did share with me some of the challenges faced by the majority of the VI in terms of financial support during their learning years, the societal stigma attached to VI person as only fit for certain professions like performers or singers. She did emphasize whether all VI people born in India can access the empowerment given through the well-known launch pad, 'higher education' in leading universities/ institutions. Beyond the obstacle of getting in to an institution the VI person faces the challenges in the library that are equipped with resource materials in the form of books stacked in high shelves. A mere audio speaker wired to the computer would suffice for the VI person to identify the books but without the help of the Staff or friends he cannot identify and borrow the books he/she needs, so their assigned work is totally dependent on the peer or friends literally at others disposal. Moreover the Accession numbers are not in Braille format for them identify the book. Even if the libraries and universities do provide certain facilities to bridge the gap, the access is installed by a person who has visual dominance that it exhibits to be the least user -friendly to the VI person.

More so ever is the hurdle of getting acceptance at the peer level, to guide and share joys and sorrows together. It is because the peers look more often about their shortcomings rather than their strengths. Their presence in the university with its sprawling building and varied terrains not only confuses the VI person but also a stranger to the place and more dependent on his peers and friends.

Finally the last challenge the VI people face is their learning becomes difficult even inside the classrooms. We are aware that mostly all faculty members use power point presentation or the white board in higher education. Or at least the chalk board which is of no use or less use to the VI persons, and very few lecturers upload their lecture notes so taking down notes or jotting down the points becomes difficult as we know that not all VI people are good at memorising lectures like our Dr. Sivaraman of Presidency College. Special committees and units established in the University and colleges shall ensure that every building including faculty, colleges and student activity centers provides basic facilities as well as specific facilities for the VI students in accordance with universal design guidelines.

- Specialized Walkways: These should have tactile paving or detectable warning surfaces to alert visually impaired individuals of hazards or changes in direction. The surfaces should contrast with the surrounding area to aid in navigation.

- Elevators: Elevators should have braille or tactile buttons for floor selection and audible announcements for each floor to assist those with visual impairments.

- Toilets: Accessible toilets should be equipped with features like grab bars, tactile signage indicating the door's use, and clear signage to locate them easily.

- Car Parks: Designated accessible parking spots should have clear signage with tactile markings indicating their location. They should also be located close to entrances for ease of access.

- Slopes: Slopes instead of stairs or steps should have handrails and tactile markings at the top and bottom to indicate the transition.

- Tactile Blocks: Tactile blocks should be installed at the edges of platforms, walkways, and stairs to warn visually impaired individuals of potential hazards.

- Clear Signage: Signage should have high contrast lettering and symbols for better visibility. Braille should be provided alongside visual information for those who are blind or have low vision.

By incorporating these features into the design of public spaces, we can ensure that visually impaired individuals can navigate their surroundings safely and independently. We being the more rationalised beings should be able to understand the difficulties faced by the visually impaired, how many of the institutions and colleges provide these facilities to the visually impaired. Thus their learning through description would not be sufficed to lead them to their desired destination.

There are several other things that need to be catered to for the well-being of the VI more than their mobility alone; it covers more of their emotional needs. People around them are sensitized in such a way that they would not take the VI for granted but be person who can really be a pillar support through thick and thin. Many of the VI finds it difficult especially the women while choosing their life- partners. Though the gender difference need not be mentioned as such both male and female find it difficult while choosing the life partners. In the existing degrees of unknown factors it cannot be taken for granted to raise a family. Here, a good associative buddies who are chivalrous at heart can play vital role in taking part as a well-wisher and help the VI person and their gifted partners. We must be clear and not be carried away by the movies and mass media portrayals that the life is so rosy and liveable for all VI person. A part of the world that is not so friendly to normal women themselves how hard would it be to deprive of the vision that can lead them to needless pitfalls.

Though I have pointed out the difficulties of the VI persons, I am not completely negative about their life in this world would be difficult always. We, people with gift of vision can join hands in sharing the world amicably along with the VI persons. Some of the initiatives that have been rightly developed are the apps that could give auditory answers for the questions raised by the VI persons. Many of my students gather together and were able to arrange a sports day in college where only the VI students participated. Their organizing skills and elocutionary skills were exhibited rightly; of course with the help of some of the faculty members of which Mr Vikas of the department of English proved it to be. There will always be a Thamarai Selvan who is excellent in culling out the programmes of the government and G.O.'s and shares it among all; a Rangarajan who can move your heart with his mellifluous voice singing some great songs; or a Pandian who capably found a place in the forest department are still on my contact list. Be it my students or colleagues, it is for us to be the members who can empathize and understand their difficulties. Until then these Champions of LIGHT are forced to be marginalised and their voices yet to be heard by all authorities of all fields.

Reference

Galiano, A.R., Portalier, S. (2010). Audio description, practice and research Modelling, Measurement and Control A. AMSE Press, vol. 71, 3-4, 128-135.

Gleitman, L. (1990). The structural sources of verb meaning. Language Acquisition, 1, 3-55.

Russell, B. (1965). The Problems of Philosophy. London: Thornton Butterworth.

Vygotsky, L.S. (1962). Thought and Language. Cambridge, MA: MIT Press.

Scope Of Visually Challenged People In Banking Sector:

Aravind Rajendran
Banker

Introduction.

Being a backbone of our economy, Banking sector plays a pivotal role in making money, reach from surplus area to the people in need there by, accelerating the economic activity.

Thus, it enables employment generation, increase in the production of goods and services and ensure sustainable improvement in our society.

Visually challenged bankers also play a significant role in the evolution of banking sector through out the world.

Especially, the computerization and digitization of banking industry, which began in India in the 1990S, made banking services more accessible and affordable to the visually challenged people and generated huge employment opportunities apart from the regular teaching jobs.

However, as change is inevitable, the recent technological improvements brought a series of disruptive changes in the employment market, which has resulted in a lot of challenges in getting employment itself especially for visually challenged aspirants.

Hence, let us discuss the scope of visually challenged people in the banking sector in the near future which will help us all, be ready for the upcoming opportunities.

Jobs performed in the past generation.

During the pre-economic reform days when, banking was happening only through physical files, visually challenged people had very limited scope like attending telephone calls and transferring to the respective authorities.

In fact, there was a special post "Telecall operator" where banking jobs are identified specially for visually challenged employees.

Apart from transferring calls, VI employees solved customer queries, gave products related awareness and few people contributed in bank's legal aspects also.

After the computerization and THE enactment of "PERSONS WITH DISABILITIES ACT, 1995", more jobs were identified and VI employees started giving significant contribution especially to marketing and finance departments through follow-up and report preparation.

This resulted in many banks, having documented the list of jobs, which can be done by VI employees.

However, since this documentation has to be an ongoing process, let us understand the expected changes, which will affect the banking industry in the near future.

Expected changes in banking sector in the future

1. Automation of routine jobs.

As we are witnessing already, the jobs, which are repetitive by nature are getting automatized through sophisticated softwares.

2. AI tools.

The recent explosion of artificial intelligent tools enables the banks do data management and customer service with lessor human strength.

3. Banking inside customer's pockets.

The concept of banking itself is shifting from banking premises into customer's mobile handsets and wearable devises, which has the potential to make land lines and computers redundant shortly.

Hence, time has come for VI employees to re-skill and upskill themselves to utilize these changes to their upliftment.

Hence, let us discuss the important characteristics to be developed from our side to withstand these changes and remain competitive in this field.

Expected characteristics by the banking industry from the employees.

1. Become an active customer.

As we require banking to be more accessible, VI people have to use all of the banking services from the customer's point of view using their mobiles and wearables right from their school days when accounts are opened for them.

Especially, the recent technical products like WhatsApp banking, Digital currency apps, and CPPS have to be used by VI people as they are expected to be their preferred future payment modes.

Then only, they can identify and point out the issues in those products to the banks and resolve their accessibility concerns at the earliest.

Such experiences can enable them to understand the grievance redressal mechanisms of their bank and guide customers properly when they become employees.

2. Considering problematic situations as big opportunities.

Every experienced banker knows that angry customers are the best potential source of business.

As banking has gone inside the customer's pockets, public approach the employees only when they face any big issue or incur any financial loss.

Hence, such instances have to be considered as the best opportunities to interact with customers, understand their business requirements and recommend the appropriate products.

3. Diversified knowledge.

Continuous upgradation of our skills through clear understanding of the current affairs is a must for all to understand various types of customer needs and pitch the suitable products for them.

Hence, VI people are expected to identify the right accessible sources through which, they can develop their basic understanding in many fields using the assistive technologies.

I personally recommend the online libraries like "Kindle" or "Bookshare" for reading books and magazines like "Madras paper" for understanding current affairs around the world using screen readers like talkback, voiceover or NVDA easily.

There is a serious fear of job loss due to the arrival of AI tools through out the world which necessitates the clear understanding of the way, knowledge is absorbed differently by men related to machines.

There are three types of learning through which, we attain knowledge in any field.

i.   Logical learning.

ii. Imaginary learning.

iii. Intuitive learning.

Any powerful data analytics tool can work only through logical learning, which is predicting future using the existing data obtained from the recorded customer transactions.

On the other hand, men only can utilize their intuitive thinking through imagination using such data and identify the upcoming business opportunities and the right customers for maximizing the profits for the organisation.

Hence, VI employees are expected to learn the techniques like "Prompt engineering", to give effective commands to the AI softwares to extract the required data in the proper form for effective decision making purpose.

Conclusion

"The man who asks a question is a fool for a minute, the man who does not ask is a fool for life" is the popular saying of Confucius.

Hence, let us improve the habit of learning through questioning in a humble way to the right people and adapt ourselves to the changes and expectations of the world on the daily basis.

Why I Like The Temple (Poem)

Ashwin Saravanan
Grade 11

Because it is all right to be in a good mood there,

Forgetting the sorrows of life for a while,

Thinking only of the lord,

And filling our minds with pleasant memories.

I like the way the temple grants permission for expressing one's feelings

-A mother grieving about an unborn child,

And another, thanking the lord upon the fulfillment of their desires.

I don't like the clanging of the bells,

Or the Prashad being thrown away in the wastebasket,

Or the people thronging the temple in large numbers

To seek the blessings of the lord.

But I like the way some people

Spend their time in the temple by meditating before the lord,

Reflecting on the sins committed,

And seeking forgiveness from the lord.

The Ruined House (Story)

An old man wearing tattered clothes sat in an armchair in his house. His wife stood near by, stirring a pot of stew on the burner. It was dusk. Lights began turning on in the streets. Next to the old man's house was a ruined house. Its windows were dilapidated, thick ivy hung on the walls. The garden was unkempt, the flowers drooped. Loaves of stale and mouldy bread, a saucepan, knives, cracked plates lined the shelves. In another room the shelves lining the room were full of books – books of brave warriors, of brave and daring sailors and many more. The bedroom and the bathrooms emitted a fowl smell of having not been used for a long period of time. The house had a tower built into it. The staircase to the tower spiralled of steeply. The tower overlooked the sea, and hence it was a breathtaking view.

Presently, the old man's wife called out, " Your high tea is ready."

"Coming" the man replied. He ate his high-tea with gusto, listened to the news for a while, doused the lights and went to sleep. One day, the old man did not know why he had awoken. He had just had a nightmare of a figure darting through the bushes and entering the ruined house. He went back to sleep, thinking it was just a nightmare. The next night, he awoke the same way. The unmistakable sound of the rustling twigs was heard in the silence of the night. By the time the old man marched to the window, the rustling had stopped.

The following night, the man decided to be awake in case the sound was heard again. He therefore, had a good sleep in the afternoon and was wide awake as night approached. His wife went to sleep. The old man sat next to the window.

In the middle of the night, the old man saw, a furtive figure darting towards the house. The old man followed at a safe distance so as not to attract the suspect's attention. The intruder entered the house, sauntered towards the bookshelf and began pulling down the books. He began to thumb through them with a flashlight. The man continued his reading for about an hour, replaced the books on the shelf and walked out. The next night, the old man saw lights flashing in the ruined house. He went out to investigate. He saw, a pearly white figure, darting through the house, and climbing the spiral staircase. The suspect ran up, withdrew a flashlight from his pocket and began signalling to someone out at sea. The person at sea responded back. The old man standing below the staircase of the tower was a retired detective. He at once recognised it as morse code. The code was a piece of cake for the old man to crack. He got the following message :

"Send word to Black Parrot. Cargo not yet received." The next morning, the old detective, walked to the docks and saw the frater 'The Black Parrot' tied to the pier. The detective glanced at the cargo nets. He saw, several crates lowered down onto the dock. One of the shoreman accidently opened one of the crates by using a screw driver. Out tumbled several rapped packages of banknotes worth a fortune!

"You" shouted one of the men. "Why did you open it in front of everyone?"

"My mistake."

 "I was asked to open one of the crates. With so many crates, I must have opened the wrong crate." The detective overheard all this. He silently went to a nearby drugstore and called the cops. Within minutes, a police car reached the docks. The police officer saw the packages of banknotes and exclaimed,

"Amazing! We have been hunting for this loot. Thanks to you sir, we have a fortune and a clever ring of thieves."

"It was nothing, officer," the detective replied, blushing.

"I don't know how to express my gratitude. Just ask anything and you shall have it."

"Officer, it would be grateful if the ruined house near my house could be a tourist attraction. People would love to see it."

"I shall ask my men to repair the building slightly so it is safe for people to go and visit."

"Excellent! Thank you so much, officer."

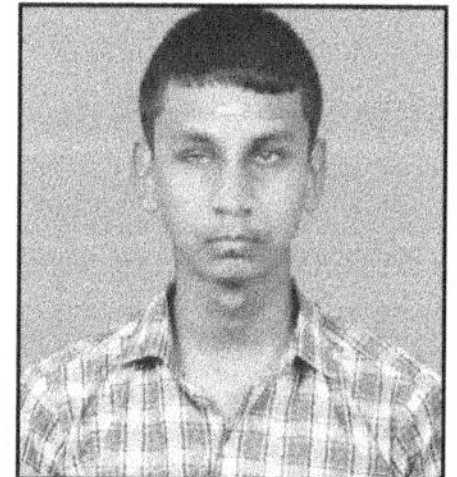

Ashwin Saravanan , *Ashwin Saravanan, a grade 11 student studying in ISC curriculum with subjects Biology, Environmental Sciences, Business Studies, Commerce, English. He is an ardent lover of devotional music, travelling visiting temples, historical monuments. He enjoys savouring variety of dishes local to the place where he is travelling. He wishes to pursue a career in Environmental sciences.*

Making Of A Specially Abled Doctor.

Dr. Hitesh Prasad B. BAMS M.D. (Ayu)

It wasn't easy to learn everything from beginning, I had to accept the new life, new reality and establish the new identity. I am a Doctor with different abilities.

I'm Dr. Hitesh, a visually impaired Ayurveda Physician and Assistant Professor from Karnataka. Yes, you heard it right, I am a doctor with visual impairment. By the way, can a visually impaired become a doctor in India? Are you also a visually challenged wishing to be a Doctor in India?? Then definitely you should listen to my story.

I was born to a consanguineous couple, meaning my parents were close blood relatives even before their marriage. Perhaps due to this, I developed a rare eye disease called Retinitis Pigmentosa, which causes progressive deterioration of vision as one grows older. I experienced difficulty seeing during my early childhood, but it was corrected with spectacles. I still remember being the only one in my primary school wearing large glasses. Later, in 5th standard, I was selected for Jawahar Navodaya Vidyalaya, an event that completely changed the course of my life. During my seven years at Navodaya, I experienced ups and downs and made major adaptations in my life—I entered as a sighted child but left as a blind one.

I was 13 years old when I first realized I felt uneasy at night. Initially, I thought this was normal for everyone, but I soon realized I wasn't as comfortable as my friends in doing things at night. I was surprised to see them riding bicycles effortlessly in the dark, something I struggled with despite being a good rider during the day. After many falls and injuries, it became clear that I had lost my vision in the dark. I was too young to fully understand what was happening to me, but I was fortunate to receive my education in a place that was more than a school—it was like a temple.

My friends never bullied me or laughed at me when I fell or bumped into walls. This level of kindness is not often the case for children with conditions similar to mine. My first dependency began with my friends, who defended me in vulnerable situations. Even though I couldn't see the blackboard from the front bench, they would dictate to me, making sure I didn't miss anything. During the compulsory morning jog, I would run while holding onto their shoulders. Frequent falls and injuries gradually kept me away from sports, but I developed a passion for reading novels, which made many friends gravitate towards me to hear stories. This continued until I completed my 10th standard. Despite my struggles, my difficulties remained unknown to my parents. However, during the summer holidays, when I was without my friends, I couldn't hide my challenges. Initially, my parents scolded me for my unusual behavior at night, but I would cover it up with made-up stories the next morning.

Eventually, my parents noticed my night-time visual difficulty—it was as if I had been caught. They took me to Narayana Eye Hospital in Bangalore, one of the renowned eye hospitals at the time. I underwent numerous diagnostic tests, visiting almost every day for a week. The diagnosis was devastating: I was suffering from a rare eye disease that would gradually take away all of my vision, and there was no treatment available at the time. They advised us to obtain a Disability Certificate, for which I was eligible. This news broke my parents deeply. We stayed at a cousin's home in Bangalore, and for the first time, I saw both my parents cry together. Surprisingly, the diagnosis didn't have a deep emotional impact on me. Soon, my vacations were over, and I returned to school, which was perhaps the most comforting place for me.

My studies became significantly more challenging during my 11th and 12th grades. I had to rely on a table lamp and torchlight for evening studies and would sit on the open terrace under sunlight during the day. One positive aspect was that sports and jogging were exempted for 12th-grade students to allow more focus on academics. This spared me many embarrassing and discriminatory situations that I had previously faced during sports hours. Things went on smoothly only because of the friends who shared their shoulders in saving me from all kinds of difficulties. I successfully completed my 12th grade with a good score and aspired to pursue a career in medicine. However, this marked the beginning of the darker days of my life. In the secure hostels of Navodaya, surrounded by friends, I had never imagined a life of dependency. I joined for crash course tuition to NEET & JEE exams in Mysuru, it was the first year of launch of NEET & JEE and I qualified both the exams. I decided to pursue a medical degree.

Very recently, the Supreme Court had imposed stringent regulations for visually challenged individuals pursuing medical courses. I had to undergo a fitness test to qualify for the MBBS program. Unfortunately, only a few reputed eye hospitals conducted this test, and none were located in Karnataka. As a result, I had to travel to Mumbai for my fitness certificate. I vaguely remember visiting JJ Hospital, where I was denied permission to pursue medicine. I was utterly confused and lacked any contacts for guidance. I reached out to higher authorities through emails but received no response. In the meantime, I submitted my options for B.Tech admissions through JEE and was allotted a seat in the Information Technology branch at the National Institute of Technology, Karnataka, Surathkal. With no hope left for medicine, I joined engineering. However, those five months at NITK were the most challenging period of my life. I struggled to adapt to the elite environment due to my deep-rooted inferiority complex. I couldn't find a friend who could help me by dictating what was written on the board or by offering support when needed. I felt completely broken. It was during this difficult time that I received an SMS from the Karnataka Examination Authority announcing that seats for Ayurveda studies were now available. This message felt like a lifeboat to me. Given the rapid deterioration of my vision, I believed Ayurveda would be the best choice for both my treatment and career. I submitted my options and was allotted a free seat at the Government Ayurveda Medical College, Mysore. Without informing anyone, I left NITK and joined the Ayurveda program in Mysore. I decided to stay in a hostel again, but this time, I was vulnerable to bullying and mockery from my hostel mates. One of the greatest challenges for partially blind individuals is that they often do not disclose their difficulties, which makes it impossible for others to understand their struggles without being told. To the external world, I appeared normal but lacking in confidence, which was far from the truth.

My next challenge was to pursue a five-year course without knowing what the future held. My vision was deteriorating rapidly, and it became clear that I couldn't follow the conventional methods of studying. Reading books became difficult for me. Then came the digital world, which transformed my life and brought me to where I am today. Smartphones and laptops deserve much of the credit for supporting my studies. During most practicals and clinicals, where I couldn't see with the naked eye, I captured images with my smartphone and magnified them to study. I read books in PDF format, utilizing the dark mode and negative mode features to convert white backgrounds to black, which was far more comfortable for prolonged reading. Projectable microscopes helped me view slides during physiology and pathology studies. I also stored images of important specimens on a pen drive, which I transferred to my laptop to view them in an enlarged format whenever needed. The 3D Human Body Android app and Acland's video lectures made anatomy much easier for me. Non-clinical and theoretical subjects of my course went smoothly, thanks to technology. However, learning bedside examinations and clinical skills was more challenging. By then, LED-based sphygmomanometers had been introduced, which were a blessing. Digital speaking BP apparatuses also became available. Nowadays, most medical reports are provided in PDF format as soft copies, and applications like Google Lens and Lookout assist me in reading paper reports. Speech-to-text applications have made me a faster typist than some of my sighted classmates.

By the time I reached my final year, many video lectures were available on YouTube, which served as excellent alternatives to reading textbooks. I carried a table lamp to write my exams, and the compensatory time provided by universities was a great boon, enabling me to compete with my sighted peers. I developed myself into a good academician, public health speaker, and column writer. I remain a versatile reader through audiobook applications like Bookshare, Sugamya Pustakalaya, and Audible, which have allowed me to continue reading Kannada and English novels. With special permission, I pursued my master's degree soon after completing my undergraduate studies. Technology enabled me to rank among the toppers in my university and earn an MD in Ayurveda Community Medicine.

The COVID-19 crisis helped me become a telemedicine consultant. The digitization of healthcare services allowed me to maximize my abilities. During this time, I also learned to use NVDA and JAWS through Mitra Jyoti. Online courses offered by Enable India helped me master Microsoft Office. Encounters with visually challenged doctors like Sharad Philip, Meghana, and Preeti through Eyeway inspired me to work seamlessly. During my postgraduate studies, I developed a keen interest in statistics and SPSS. I successfully completed two cross-sectional research surveys with the help of Google Forms and published five research papers in international peer-reviewed journals. I regularly write Kannada health awareness columns in popular magazines. Additionally, I am a blogger who publishes health awareness articles. I also run a YouTube channel dedicated to Kannada literature, with around 1.5k subscribers. I lend my voice to Kannada awareness videos for Eyeway. Thanks to technology, I no longer see myself as blind. I have honed various skills during my studies. Today, I am not only an Assistant Professor at a private medical college but also an online consultant. I rely heavily on digital tools that enhance my counseling and diagnostic skills. I am also learning Naadi Pariksha, a special examination skill in Ayurveda, which will undoubtedly improve my clinical expertise. This is my story. I don't claim it's impossible for a visually challenged person to become a doctor, but it's certainly not easy. There are numerous legal restrictions, and many laws regarding medical education for the visually challenged lack clarity and are open to subjective interpretation. There is a strong need for legal reforms and greater awareness regarding medical education for the visually disabled.

Dr. Hitesh Prasad, *is a Visually Challenged and Specially abled Ayurveda Physician, UG - B.A.M.S from Govt. Ayurveda Medical College, Mysuru and PG - M.D. (Ayu) from Govt. Ayurveda Medical College, Mysuru. He is also a Teacher, Wellness Guide, Diet & Lifestyle counselor, Yoga Trainer, Public Speaker, Author, Columnist, Blogger, Digital Content Creator and a Versatile Reader, and also a Singer, Storyteller and Dancer. A passionate teacher of varying subjects, committed to be creative, productive and innovative, and aspiring to serve my motherland.*

State of Visually Impaired
in 75 Years of Independent India:
Issues and Challenges

Review of assistive technology for visually impaired issues and challenges:

B. Kannan

Introduction:

Disability can be conquered by strong will, hard work and with the help of assistive technology.

When man began to record their views, ideas, thoughts and experiences the practice of writing was born. Languages developed and literature flourished. Arithmetic knowledge improved that paved way for various fields such as science, economics, commerce Etc.

Difficulty for VI in olden days:

But education and acquiring knowledge were very difficult for the visually impaired as they could not read and write like abled people. This was the situation for many centuries with few exceptions.

Braille Writing System:

This situation was changed by one great invention called the "braille" read/write system, developed by Louise Braille, a French man.

Really this "braille" method is the great boon to visually impaired community. Thousands of visually impaired persons got education all over the world because of this braille method.

Development of braille in India:

Braille, the tactile writing system for visually impaired people, has a fascinating history in India.

Braille was introduced in India in the mid-19th century by Christian missionaries and educators who were inspired by Louis Braille's work. The first Braille press in India was established in 1889 by a British missionary named Thomas Rhodes, in Bombay (now Mumbai).

Many special schools for the visually impaired were established by them. School for the blind Palayankottah and St. Xaviors school for the blind, Bombay were some of the popular schools.

Efforts were made to standardize Braille in Indian languages. The National Institute for the Visually Handicapped (NIVH), government of India, Dehradun, established in the year 1952, was instrumental in this regard. It has worked on developing Braille codes for various Indian languages to ensure blind individuals have access to education and literature in their native languages.

Regional braille press was established in Chennai to print school books in south Indian languages.

National Association for the Blind India, established in the same year 1952 established a braille press in Mumbai and printed a lot of English and Hindi books.

The National Federation of the Blind India and All India Confederation of the Blind have played vital role in braille book production.

Braille lending libraries were established by NIVH, NAB, NFB AND AICB for the visually impaired readers. Braille books were sent to visually impaired persons across the country.

Indian postal department helped to this mission by sending the braille books across the country.

"Literature for the Blind, Postage Free" were the golden words for the blind, given in Post Office Guide, Section 129/130.

Challenges: Despite the progress, size and volume of braille books, limited availability of Braille materials in regional languages, and the high cost of Braille printing devices are the big challenges in braille book production.

The refreshable braille display devises such Orbit Reader20, Braille me, HIMS Braille are some of the popular advancements in the field of braille system.

These devices can be used as stand alone readers, display devices along with computer and mobile phone screen readers and also as braille note takers.

The learning ability of the visually impaired will increase when we use braille in all our studies.

Audio materials:

Audio cassettes introduced in late 80s were the great source of learning for the visually impaired. Students recorded their study materials through voluntary readers.

Talking book libraries were established and audio cassettes were produced by the above mentioned organisations for nominal fee.

Computers are great boon to visually impaired:

Visually impaired persons were excellent in manual typewriting. However, when the computers were introduced widely in the year 1998-1999, with Windows98 Operating System, it was of the general opinion of the general public that blind persons cannot operate computers and the visually impaired employees were the burden for the government offices. We are not even allowed to touch the computer keyboard.

At the advent of Windows2000, "narrator" the inbuilt speech support in PCs draw the attention of visually impaired persons.

Henter-Joice INC, later known as "Freedom Scientific INC" introduced the powerful screen reader popularly known as "JAWS" [Job Access with Speech] in the year 2000-2001.

The NIVH, government of India institute, as well as organisations such as NAB India, NFB and AICB provided training for the visually impaired students as well as the VI employees in computer operation with the screen reader JAWS and MS Office usage such as Microsoft Word, Microsoft Excel, Microsoft PowerPoint Etc.

Scanning and Reading software:

"Open Book" software of Freedom Scientific INC, and Kurzweil1000 software of Kurzweil Educational Systems are the popular scanning and reading software for the visually impaired.

We converted thousands of pages of printed materials as accessible soft copy with the help of PC and flat bed scanner with the help of these software and acquired knowledge.

Visually impaired persons are taught to use Internet and Email with the help of JAWS effectively with the help of screen readers by NGOs such KVTC, Nethrodaya, IAB, NAB and many other organisations along with visually impaired volunteers.

NVDA Free and Open Source screen reader:

The cost of JAWS software is very high. Educational institutions and government offices are not in a position to afford to JAWS software for very high price. At this situation "NVDA" [Non Visual Desktop Access" free and open source screen reader was introduced in the year 2006. NVDA with E-Speak Speech synthesizer gained popularity as it can read in all regional languages of the world even though the voice is little bit robotic.

The Advent of Android and IOS mobile phones:

Mobile Speak and Nuance Talks and Zooms screen readers were used by us in Symbion mobile phones at the beginning of this century. These phones had keypad, easy to use and the screen reader will read the caller name/number and SMS messages to us.

Android and Iphones were introduced in the year 2012. These phones does not have physical keypad and visually impaired users faced problems in operating these touch mobile phones.

However, with the mobile phone screen readers such as Google /talk-back for Android known as "Android Accessibility Suite" and Voiceover for IOS devices our visually impaired persons excel in the optimum utilization of touch mobiles.

Now we are able to actively participate in social media such WhatsApp, Facebook, Instagram, YouTube and Twitter also known as X platform.

Mobile phone camera and Artificial Intelligence:

The mobile phone camera empowered with artificial intelligence AI technology, helps the visually impaired persons like human eyes.

The images captured through mobile camera is processed by the AI technology and VI people understand the things around them. The mobile phone can read out the printed materials, handwritten materials and name boards to the visually impaired persons.

Popular AI Apps for the visually impaired persons:

Google look out, Sullivan +, Envision AI, seeing AI by Microsoft, are some of the popular mobile AI Apps for the blind which use the phone camera to intelligently view and announce the detailed information to the visually impaired.

Supersense AI is a paid mobile AI App.

MANI is Indian currency note identifying App for the visually impaired. This App is free.

Cash Reader is a paid App to identify the currency notes of various countries including India.

Smart Glasses for the visually impaired:

The mobile camera and artificial intelligence are combined and smart glasses are introduced recently.

OrCam and Envision AI glasses are the international products in this category.

Smart Vision Glasses, Drishti, Jyoti AI are the popular products manufactured in India.

A small camera is fixed in the normal spectacles and the camera communicate with our mobile phones and the AI App process the images and inform us things around us, currency identification, object recognition, colour recognition and face recognition.

These smart glasses are very expensive and the manufacturers do not tell the configuration of the products publicly.

Conclusion:

No doubt if correctly used, technology will complement our skill and abilities and empower us to lead a very dignified and successful life along without sighted friends and relatives happily.

Navigating the intersection of Visual Impairment & Artificial Intelligence:

A Deep Dive into Empowerment, Prospects & Future Challenges

Smt. Nikita Raut & Shri Sameer Latey

Abstract:

The ongoing developments in Artificial Intelligence (AI) have created the possibility of developing new solutions to increase accessibility, autonomy, and inclusion for Visually Impaired (V I) individuals. In this paper, we have tried to visualize possible AI-assisted solutions in the fields of education, employment, and independent living.

Artificial Intelligence can provide accessible interactive learning products that would raise the overall quality of the learning experience of V I students and greatly improve their learning outcomes. In addition, these products will make it possible for V I students to pursue areas of study that are considered out-of-bounds due to a lack of accessible educational material.

AI-powered screen readers and voice-controlled interfaces in the workplace can enhance accessibility in the workplace enabling the V I employees to compete for jobs on par with their sighted counterparts and enable them to access a wider range of job opportunities.

But the development of AI is a double-edged sword and if care is not taken, the developments in Artificial Intelligence can result in further marginalization of V I individuals. In the second part of this paper, we have suggested steps or precautions to be taken to ensure that the negative effects are minimized. These precautions include taking care that the training material used to train AI tools is free of biases against persons with visual impairment, integrating inclusive development principles in the development of AI tools right from the inception stage, and ensuring that the AI tools are affordable.

Keywords:

Artificial Intelligence (AI), Education , Employment, Accessibility, Inclusivity

Contents

1 Introduction

    1.1 What is AI

    1.2 Importance of AI in supporting the blind

2   Benefits of AI for the blind

    2.1 In Jobs

        2.1.1   AI powered tools that enhance job opportunities for the blind

        2.1.2   Role of inclusive design in creating job opportunities

    2.2 In Education

        2.2.1   AI applications that support learning & accessibility

        2.2.2   Impact of voice assistance & text-to-speech technologies on education

        2.2.3   How AI can provide personalised learning experiences

3   Pitfalls of AI for the blind

    3.1 In Jobs

        3.1.1   Risk of over-reliance on AI & potential job displacement

        3.1.2   Challenges in ensuring AI inclusivity & workplace integration

        3.1.3   Need for continuous learning & adaptation to new AI tools

    3.2 In Education

        3.2.1   Digital divide & access to AI resources

        3.2.2   Ensuring data security & privacy for users

4   Balancing the Equation

    4.1 Strategies for maximising benefits while minimising risks

    4.2 User-centered design & stakeholder involvement in AI development

    4.3 Future prospects & ongoing research in AI for the blind

5   Conclusion

1. INTRODUCTION:

1.1 What is AI?

With the launch of Chat GPT, the term, Artificial Intelligence, entered into public use. Today, we have many AI driven resources including Gemini, Claude AI etc. But let us first understand the meaning of the term AI.

The Encyclopedia Britannica defines the term, Artificial Intelligence (AI) as " the ability of a digital computer or computer-controlled robot to perform tasks commonly associated with intelligent beings." (1)

The term, AI is frequently applied to projects aimed at developing systems which have processes similar to intellectual processes in humans including the ability to reason, discover meaning, generalize or learn from past experience.

1.2 Importance of AI in supporting the blind

AI has emerged as a powerful & versatile tool for empowering the blind. AI powered tools can improve the quality of life & opportunities for the blind in many fields including jobs & education. Some of the benefits of AI for the blind include

a. Voice assistants which enable speech-based interaction with digital devices

b. Real-time object recognition to provide a picture of one's surroundings, people & text.

c. Navigation & mobility by providing step-by-step directions to reach one's destination & real-time obstacle detection

d. Translating text into braille using electronic braille readers for braille users & converting braille into normal text to facilitate communication with non-blind people

e. AI powered wearable devices including smart glasses to provide real-time descriptions of one's environment

f. AI powered educational tools make educational material accessible allowing blind students to participate in classroom discussions & online courses

g. AI powered virtual assistants & chatbots provide emotional support reducing feelings of loneliness among the blind.

In summary, AI tools provide immense help to the blind enabling them to participate on par with their non-blind colleagues & help in the social, financial & emotional integration of blind persons into society.

2. Benefits of AI for the blind:

2.1 In Jobs:

2.1.1 AI powered tools that enhance job opportunities for the blind:

AI powered tools have greatly increased job opportunities for the blind. These tools have increased the types of jobs that can be performed by the blind by making previously inaccessible tasks accessible & improving the effectiveness of existing accessibility solutions.

Some of the AI powered tools which will increase job opportunities in the near future include

a. Generative AI can be used for inclusive job designing enabling employers to accommodate the unique needs of blind employees. The participation of blind employees in shaping AI solutions will lead to inclusive solutions that will enhance job prospects.

b. AI powered software development tools (Gemini, Copilot, Chat GPT etc.) enable faster problem-solving, greater degree of experimentation & iterative development resulting in faster software development with lower coding errors.

c. Computer Vision-based Assistance (Neural Compute Stick – 2 & other Edge AI accelerators) assist blind users by providing real-time information about their surroundings facilitating quicker navigation & task execution.

In addition to the above AI tools, the addition of AI tools to existing accessible solutions like screenreaders have greatly increased their capabilities. For example, the addition of AI tools like Gemini with existing screenreaders like JAWS & NVDA has increased the ability of the blind to read hard-copy documents & scanned image files independently.

2.1.2 Role of Inclusive Design in creating job opportunities:

The importance of inclusive design in job opportunities cannot be over-emphasised. An inclusive solution helps in attracting & retaining a diverse workforce, ensures accessibility & universal solutions. Implementing accessibility features in a job design or software at the design stage also results in financial savings for the enterprise. Studies have shown that retro-fitting accessibility solutions on inaccessible softwares can cost upto 10,000 times the original development cost.

To ensure that accessibility features are properly implemented at the design stage, the developers should follow inclusive human-centric design principles. They can take the assistance of guidelines published by the World Wide Web Consortium & Microsoft. These inclusive features should include keyboard navigation, alternative text for images, voice-enabled interfaces or speech-to-text, text or image-to-speech.

2.2 Education:

2.2.1 AI applications that support learning & accessibility:

AI powered applications play an important role in enhancing accessibility of learning materials & resources for the blind. The AI powered applications make the process of generating accessible educational content easier, cheaper & faster in comparison to traditional non-AI methods. These AI powered tools promote equity, inclusion & independence in education & beyond.

Some of the AI powered tools used to increase access to education for the blind include

a. Assistive technology (Antara's Vembi Converter, Daisy Consortium etc.) converts books, journals, test papers etc. into accessible formats. These technologies also generate descriptions on-demand for images & are also used to describe complex diagrams & charts.

b. Innovative education tools (NWEA, Braille AI tutor etc.) enhance accessibility in areas with previously unmet accessibility needs including enhanced math accessibility, teaching braille through gamification, provision of educational materials using audio & augmented reality etc.

c. Inclusive design (I-STEM etc.) enhances document accessibility including complex layouts & scientific terminology by combining AI with human corrections.

2.2.2 Impact of voice assistance & text-to-speech technologies on education:

Voice assistance & Text-to-speech technologies (TTS) have greatly increased the accessibility of educational resources & made it more engaging. Voice assistance & TTS technologies enable personalized learning, collaboration in learning benefiting both students & educators.

Some of the benefits of these technologies to blind students are given below.

a. Voice Assistance technologies including smart speakers (Alexa, Google Dot etc.) allow students to learn at their own speed without external pressure. Students can get help in completing their homework, have stories read to them, listen to audio books & access information online. Collaborative voice assistance solutions enable collaborative discussion among students facilitating discussion & knowledge sharing.

b. Text-to-speech (TTS) enhance accessibility by converting text content into spoken language. Educators can leverage the use of AI TTS solutions to provide diverse auditory learning options for students. Multilingual Text-To-Speech (TTS) solutions help make educational materials available across language barriers & reach a wider audience.

2.2.3 How AI can provide a personalized learning experience:

AI's ability to quickly analyse vast amounts of data & draw actionable results from such analysis helps in creating learning experiences tailored to the needs, interests & tastes of each individual student. AI powered tools put the student at the centre of the learning journey & enhances engagement, relevance & success of the educational journey.

AI powered educational tools create a personalized educational experience by performing the following steps

a. AI powered tools analyse the student's needs, interests etc. & generate personalized learning paths by adapting the educational content, instructional strategies & pace of learning to suit each student's unique needs.

b. Adaptive learning technologies use AI based algorithms to analyse student performance data & adjust the instruction accordingly providing personal feedback & scaffolding to promote mastery of skills.

c. AI driven analytics are used by educators to make informed choices about the content & method of instruction & allocate resources effectively. These analytical tools also enable the teachers to pinpoint areas where the student is struggling or excelling & optimize individualized lesson plans.

3. Pitfalls of AI for the blind:

3.1 In Jobs:

3.1.1 Risk of over-reliance on AI & potential job displacement:

AI is rapidly becoming an integral part of our daily life. We are surrounded by AI powered gadgets & solutions from virtual assistants like Siri & Alexa to predictive text when typing messages or documents. Advances in AI hold the promise of introducing self-driving cars in the near future.

The integration of AI solutions in the workplace has the potential to revolutionise industries by boosting efficiency & unleashing creativity. AI powered automation will streamline repetitive tasks allowing employees to focus on higher-value work that requires critical-thinking & problem-solving skills. This shift in job roles enables employees to tap into their full potential & contributes to overall workforce transformation.

But this rosy picture also holds several dangers, especially for blind employees. The dangers to blind employees for the implementation of AI solutions are given below.

a. The spread of AI will lead to the replacement of employees by AI solutions in traditional jobs in sectors including manufacturing, healthcare, finance etc. The implementation of AI solutions is likely to affect the jobs generally held by blind individuals disproportionately.

b. The replacement of human workers by AI solutions will lead to a larger pool of prospective employees chasing a shrinking pool of jobs which may result in further marginalisation of the blind individuals.

c. The loss of employment will result in lower economic power leading to reduction in spending which may further disadvantage the blind individuals.

d. Blind employees who have lost their jobs & are unable to find new ones will be forced to depend on family members or charities for meeting their daily needs. This dependence can lead to disagreements among family members, substance abuse & mental problems.

3.1.2 Challenges in ensuring AI inclusivity & workplace integration:

The integration of AI solutions in the workplace presents both opportunities & challenges with regard to diversity, equality & inclusion strategies. Some of the challenges posed by AI powered solutions to inclusivity, diversity & equity activities are given below.

a. AI based tools can unintentionally perpetuate existing inequalities by continuing marginalisation of historically marginalised groups & reducing the effectiveness of inclusion strategies. This behaviour might be due to biased historical data or flawed algorithms. AI tools trained on biased historical data would perpetuate systematic inequalities.

b. Use of AI tools in business processes including recruitment, performance evaluation, decision-making etc. can raise ethical questions. It is necessary to ensure transparency, accountability & responsible deployment of AI tools to ensure that ethical questions are effectively answered & the tools follow diversity, equality & inclusivity principles.

c. Ethically designed AI solutions can enhance inclusivity efforts. These tools can assist in diversity & inclusivity audits, workforce analysis etc. leading to equitable outcomes.

3.1.3 Need for continuous learning & adaptation to new AI tools:

The rapidly evolving landscape of AI powered tools will necessitate continuous learning & adaptation. Learning will become a lifelong activity in the new AI dominated workplace to maintain one's edge & skill set.

Some of the reasons for continuous learning in the coming AI dominated workplace are given below.

a. AI tools & techniques will evolve constantly & rapidly. Continuous learning will ensure that we are ready to take advantage of the latest technological developments.

b. Learning new AI tools will help in keeping our skills relevant in the workplace. All employees including software developers, data scientists, business professionals etc. will have to keep their skills updated or risk job loss.

c. AI tools can analyse large amounts of data & present multiple solutions to the user. Continuous learning will keep our problem-solving skills agile & enable us to select the right tool for the specific problem & select the appropriate solution from those presented by the AI tool.

d. Employers prefer professionals who keep their skills & knowledge updated. Continuous learning will help in career growth.

3.2 In Education:

3.2.1 Digital divide & access to educational resources:

Digital Divide is the gap between those countries, cities or individuals with access to information & communication technologies & those countries, cities or individuals without such access. Due to the rapid growth & deployment of AI powered tools & solutions, the digital divide is increasingly referred to as the AI divide. The AI divide arises due to the differences in AI access, skill sets, economic growth, ownership of training data used to train AI tools, development levels etc.

Addressing the AI divide & ensuring equal access to AI resources is essential for an inclusive & innovative society. Some of the steps which may be taken to bridge the AI divide are given below.

a. Digital literacy is essential for bridging the AI gap. Educators can deploy AI solutions to close or minimise the AI gap.

b. Policy makers must give priority to deploying technologies to close the AI gap.

3.2.2 Ensuring data security & privacy for users:

In the book, the Godfather, written by Mario Puzo, the Godfather, Don Corleone remarks " A lawyer with a briefcase can steal more than a hundred men with guns.". In today's digital age, a hacker who gains access to an organisation's or individual's critical data can steal a thousand times more. The misuse of a person's critical data including name, address, medical information, financial information, etc. can lead to many crimes. In the field of education, the theft of test papers or answer keys can make or break careers. The damage caused by such thefts is borne disproportionately by the marginalised sections of society including the blind.

Some of the steps which an organisation should follow to maintain data security & protect user information are given below.

a. Obtain user consent before collecting personal data & communicate in a transparent manner how such data will be used & period for which it will be retained.

b. Strictly follow relevant privacy regulations (European GDPR etc.)

c. Encrypt & anonymise personally identifiable information & use strong encryption methods when data is being transferred or at rest.

d. Implement access control measures so that access is limited to authorised persons only.

e. Conduct regular security audits & monitor implementation of security practices

f. Have well-defined protocols for handling data breaches

g. Educate users about privacy risks & best practices

h. Establish granular controls on data sharing

i. Provide users with an option to opt-out of data collection.

4. Balancing the Equation:

4.1 Strategies for maximising benefits while minimising risks:

In the foregoing sections, we have looked at the benefits to the blind from use of AI powered tools in the fields of jobs & education. We have also looked at the pitfalls in the same fields due to use of AI powered tools. Now, let us look at some strategies through which we can try to maximise the benefits of AI for the blind while at the same time minimising the risks.

a. Ensure that blind individuals are involved in all steps of the development of the AI solutions including design, testing & feedback to ensure their accessibility

b. Prioritise understanding of user needs & goals by adopting a user-centered design method

c. Ensure that the AI judgement is combined with appropriate human oversight

d. Leverage crowd sourcing for data labelling & validation

e. Ensure that the training data used to train the AI solutions is free from bias

f. Promote fairness in AI decision-making

g. Ensure privacy & data security

4.2 User-centered design & stakeholder involvement in AI development:

Adopting user-centered design & involving all stakeholders in development of AI solutions will result in solutions which are well-suited for their tasks & will not face resistance from users. We will now list some steps which should be taken to ensure the AI solutions have user-centered design & stakeholder involvement.

User-centered design –

a. Understand user needs, goals & pain points

b. Prioritise on solving the user's pain points & meeting user needs when designing & developing solutions

c. Involve the end-users in testing of each iterative design, testing & refinement

d. Prototypes should be tested with real users in real-life settings

e. Ensure accessibility to make the solutions inclusive for diverse users

Stakeholder Involvement –

a. Collaborate with all types of stakeholders including end-users, developers, domain experts etc.

b. Ensure that the collaboration is an on-going activity throughout the design & implementation process rather than a one-off event

c. Involve all stakeholders in discussions on ethical issues including elimination of conscious & unconscious bias, fairness, privacy etc.

d. Ensure that there is alignment between user needs & business requirements.

4.3 Future prospects & on-going AI research for the blind:

In this section, we are going to gaze into our crystal balls & see what new devices & solutions on-going AI research is likely to provide for the blind in the near future.

a. AI powered wearable smart glasses which use object detection, text recognition etc. to identify things in the user's surroundings real-time & convey it to the blind user using voice assistants

b. Smart phone based solutions for identifying objects, detecting obstacles, providing real-time guidance including walking directions etc.

c. Convolutional neural networks will play a vital role in solving image classification challenges for the blind

d. Expected advances in AI & robotics may lead to personal assistive robots for the blind which would enhance their safety & independence.

5. CONCLUSION:

In the previous pages, we have considered the benefits of AI for the blind in the areas of jobs & education. We have also looked at the pitfalls due to AI in the same fields. Finally, we have used our crystal ball to gaze into the future benefits of ongoing AI research.

AI has the potential to boost inclusion & open previously unthought of opportunities for the blind if developed with adequate safeguards. If AI development is done with inclusion being an afterthought, the same AI developments can turn into a curse instead of a boon.

As we move ahead to integrate AI more & more into our lives, we should ensure that it is developed with adequate guardrails. By thoughtfully harnessing AI's potential, we can build a future that is inclusive, just & empowering for all.

Smt. Nikita Raut
Assistant General Manager & Learning Head,
Bank of Baroda
Research scholar at Shri Balaji University, Pune.
E-mail: *NIKITA.PHD-307@sbup.edu.in*

Shri Sameer Latey
Manager (Finance & Accounts),
Reliance Industries Ltd.
Email: *salatey@gmail.com*

Enhancing Spatial Awareness: For the Visually Impaired

Pranav Bhaven Savla, Pavan Maiya, Daniel Marc Maani
AS/A Level - 9618 Computer Science

Enhancing Spatial Awareness:

Object Tracking Glasses for Individuals with Visual Impairments

Abstract:

Spatial awareness, the ability to perceive and understand one's relationship to the surrounding environment, is a critical skill for safe and independent navigation. For individuals with visual impairments, navigating the built environment presents unique challenges due to limited or absent visual cues. This research paper investigates the complexities of spatial awareness for the visually impaired, examining existing assistive technologies (AT) and universal design (UD) principles while identifying their limitations. It further explores the potential of emerging technologies like haptic feedback, augmented reality (AR), and smart environments to enhance spatial perception and facilitate independent navigation. The paper emphasizes the importance of community-based approaches and participatory design to ensure that solutions are tailored to the specific needs and preferences of visually impaired individuals. By fostering a deeper understanding of the challenges and opportunities in this field, this research aims to contribute to the development of innovative solutions that empower visually impaired individuals to confidently navigate their surroundings.

1. Introduction

Spatial awareness, the cognitive ability to perceive and understand one's relationship to the surrounding environment, is fundamental for safe and independent navigation. For individuals without visual impairments, this skill is primarily facilitated by visual cues. However, for the visually impaired, who rely on other sensory modalities such as auditory, haptic (touch), and proprioceptive (body awareness), navigating the built environment presents unique challenges. These challenges can range from difficulty in constructing a mental map of the surroundings to identifying and avoiding obstacles.

The impact of limited spatial awareness on the lives of visually impaired individuals is significant. Studies have shown a correlation between impaired spatial awareness and reduced mobility, increased risk of accidents, and social isolation (Harper & Shaw, 2017; La Grow & Weessies, 2016; WHO, 2014). As such, enhancing spatial awareness for this population is not merely a matter of convenience but a critical factor in improving their quality of life and ensuring equal participation in society.

In our own exploration of assistive technologies for the visually impaired, we developed a prototype pair of glasses equipped with an ultrasonic sensor and a buzzer. The sensor emitted ultrasonic waves, and the buzzer produced a beeping sound that increased in frequency as the wearer approached an object. This simple device aimed to provide real-time feedback about the proximity of obstacles, potentially enhancing spatial awareness and navigation.

This research paper aims to delve into the intricacies of spatial awareness for the visually impaired. It will examine the existing landscape of assistive technologies (AT) and universal design (UD) principles, identifying their strengths and weaknesses in addressing the challenges faced by this population. Furthermore, the paper will explore emerging technologies such as haptic feedback, augmented reality (AR), and smart environments, assessing their potential to revolutionize spatial awareness and navigation for the visually impaired.

The research will also highlight the importance of community-based approaches and participatory design in developing effective solutions. By involving visually impaired individuals in the design process, we can ensure that solutions are tailored to their specific needs and preferences, ultimately leading to more inclusive and empowering environments.

2. The Complexities of Spatial Awareness for the Visually Impaired

Spatial awareness, the cognitive ability to perceive and understand one's relationship to the surrounding environment, is fundamental for safe and independent navigation. For individuals without visual impairments, this skill is primarily facilitated by visual cues.

However, for the visually impaired, who rely on other sensory modalities such as auditory, haptic (touch), and proprioceptive (body awareness), navigating the built environment presents unique challenges.

2.1 Challenges in Perception and Orientation

The absence or severe limitation of visual information significantly impacts the way visually impaired individuals perceive and interact with their surroundings. Studies have shown that individuals with visual impairments often have difficulty constructing accurate mental maps of their environment, a crucial component of spatial awareness (Ungar, 2000). This difficulty stems from the reliance on non-visual cues, which may be less intuitive and require more cognitive effort to process.

Furthermore, the visually impaired face challenges in detecting obstacles and hazards in their path. While canes and guide dogs offer some assistance, they have limitations in range and scope. Canes primarily detect obstacles at ground level, while guide dogs, although highly trained, cannot detect every potential hazard (Blasch et al., 2009). This leaves visually impaired individuals vulnerable to unseen obstacles, increasing the risk of accidents and injuries.

Maintaining orientation and a sense of direction also pose significant challenges. Without visual landmarks, it can be difficult for visually impaired individuals to determine their position in space and navigate effectively. This can lead to disorientation, anxiety, and even accidents (Golledge, 1997).

2.2 Impact on Daily Life and Well-being

The challenges associated with spatial awareness have a profound impact on the daily lives and well-being of visually impaired individuals. Reduced mobility and independence are common consequences, as individuals may be hesitant or unable to navigate unfamiliar environments without assistance. Research has shown that visually impaired individuals are less likely to engage in physical activity and more likely to experience social isolation compared to their sighted counterparts (La Grow & Weessies, 2016).

Furthermore, the risk of accidents and injuries is significantly higher for visually impaired individuals. According to the World Health Organization (WHO, 2014), visually impaired individuals are twice as likely to experience falls as those without visual impairments. This increased risk of accidents can further limit mobility and independence, contributing to a cycle of social isolation and decreased quality of life.

2.3 The Role of Assistive Technologies and Universal Design

Assistive technologies (AT) and universal design (UD) principles have been instrumental in mitigating some of the challenges faced by visually impaired individuals. AT, such as canes, guide dogs, and electronic travel aids (ETAs), can enhance sensory input and provide guidance. For instance, ETAs utilize ultrasonic sensors, infrared beams, or laser technology to detect obstacles and provide feedback to the user through auditory or haptic signals.

Universal design principles advocate for creating environments that are inherently accessible to people with a wide range of abilities, including those with visual impairments. This involves considering factors such as lighting, color contrast, signage, and way-finding strategies. For example, high-contrast signage with large, clear fonts can make it easier for visually impaired individuals to read and understand information.

However, despite the progress made, significant gaps remain in the development and implementation of AT and UD solutions. Many existing AT devices are expensive, complex to use, or have limited functionality. UD principles are often not fully implemented in practice, leading to environments that remain inaccessible to many visually impaired individuals.

3. Current Approaches to Enhancing Spatial Awareness

Given the critical nature of spatial awareness for the visually impaired, various approaches have been developed to mitigate the challenges discussed in the previous section. These approaches can be broadly categorized into assistive technologies (AT) and universal design (UD) principles.

3.1 Assistive Technologies (AT)

Assistive technologies are devices or systems designed to aid individuals with disabilities in performing tasks that would otherwise be difficult or impossible. For the visually impaired, these technologies aim to enhance sensory input and provide guidance for navigation and interaction with the environment. Some of the most common AT for spatial awareness include:

- **White Canes**: These simple yet effective tools are used by millions of visually impaired individuals worldwide. They primarily serve to detect obstacles at ground level, providing haptic feedback through vibrations or sounds as the cane comes into contact with objects. However, their range is limited, and they do not provide information about obstacles above ground level.

- **Guide Dogs**: Guide dogs are highly trained animals that provide invaluable assistance to visually impaired individuals. They can guide their handlers around obstacles, alert them to changes in elevation, and even help them navigate complex environments like public transportation systems. However, guide dogs require extensive training and ongoing care, making them a significant commitment for users.

- **Electronic Travel Aids (ETAs):** ETAs are electronic devices that use various sensors to detect obstacles and provide feedback to the user through auditory or haptic signals Some ETAs can even provide additional information, such as the distance to an object or the direction of a sound. However, ETAs can be expensive and complex to use, and their effectiveness can be affected by environmental factors such as lighting and weather conditions.

- **Smartphone Apps:** Smartphone apps have emerged as a promising tool for enhancing spatial awareness for the visually impaired. These apps can leverage the phone's built-in sensors, such as GPS, accelerometer, and gyroscope, to provide information about the user's location, orientation, and surroundings. Some apps also use computer vision algorithms to identify objects and landmarks, providing audio descriptions or haptic feedback. However, these apps rely on the user's ability to interact with the touchscreen and require a reliable internet connection.

3.2 Universal Design (UD) Principles

Universal design (UD) is a design philosophy that advocates for creating products, environments, and systems that are usable by people with a wide range of abilities, including those with disabilities. In the context of spatial awareness for the visually impaired, UD principles aim to create environments that are inherently accessible and easy to navigate. This involves considering factors such as:

- **Lighting**: Adequate and well-distributed lighting is essential for visually impaired individuals to navigate safely and confidently. Glare and shadows should be minimized, and different lighting levels should be provided for different areas and tasks.

- **Color Contrast**: High-contrast color schemes can make it easier for visually impaired individuals to distinguish between different surfaces and objects. For example, using light-colored walls and dark-colored floors can help to define spatial boundaries and improve visibility.

- **Signage and Wayfinding**: Signage should be clear, concise, and easy to read, with large, high-contrast fonts and Braille translations. Wayfinding strategies, such as tactile paving and audio beacons, can provide additional guidance and information.

- **Tactile and Auditory Cues**: Tactile elements, such as textured surfaces and raised markings, can help visually impaired individuals to identify landmarks and navigate through spaces. Auditory cues, such as directional sounds and verbal announcements, can also provide valuable information and guidance.

3.3 Limitations of Current Approaches

While assistive technologies and universal design principles have made significant strides in enhancing spatial awareness for the visually impaired, several limitations persist. Many existing AT devices are expensive, complex to use, or have limited functionality. For example, ETAs can be bulky and difficult to carry, and their effectiveness can be limited by environmental factors such as rain or snow.

The implementation of UD principles is often inconsistent and incomplete. Many buildings and public spaces still lack basic accessibility features, such as tactile paving or high-contrast signage. Moreover, even when UD principles are implemented, they may not be sufficient to fully address the complex navigational challenges faced by visually impaired individuals.

Furthermore, both AT and UD solutions often fail to take into account the individual needs and preferences of visually impaired individuals. For example, a person with low vision may benefit from different lighting conditions than a person who is completely blind. A personalized approach that considers the unique needs of each individual is essential for creating truly inclusive and empowering environments.

4. Case Study: Ultrasonic Sensor-Based Glasses Prototype

In an effort to explore innovative solutions for enhancing spatial awareness, our research team developed a prototype pair of glasses equipped with an ultrasonic sensor and a buzzer. This prototype aimed to address the limitations of traditional white canes, which primarily detect obstacles at ground level. The glasses were designed to emit ultrasonic waves, with the buzzer producing a beeping sound that increased in frequency as the wearer approached an object. This real-time auditory feedback was intended to provide the user with a more comprehensive understanding of their immediate surroundings.

4.1 Lessons Learned

During the prototype testing phase, several key lessons were learned. Firstly, the concept of using ultrasonic sensors to provide auditory feedback for obstacle detection was validated. Users reported that the beeping sound helped them to identify obstacles in their path and navigate more confidently, especially in unfamiliar environments. This finding aligns with previous research on the effectiveness of auditory cues in enhancing spatial awareness for visually impaired individuals (Kim & Park, 2017).

However, the prototype also highlighted several limitations. The range of the ultrasonic sensor was relatively short, limiting the user's ability to detect obstacles at a distance. Additionally, the constant beeping sound could become irritating and overwhelming, especially in noisy environments. Furthermore, the prototype only provided information about obstacles directly in front of the wearer, neglecting potential hazards to the sides or above.

4.2 Challenges and Future Directions

The prototype's limitations underscore the need for further refinement and development. One potential improvement would be to incorporate multiple ultrasonic sensors with a wider field of view, enabling the detection of obstacles from various directions. Additionally, exploring alternative feedback mechanisms, such as haptic feedback through vibrations, could offer a more subtle and less intrusive way of conveying information to the user.

Integrating the ultrasonic sensor with other technologies, such as GPS and smartphone apps, could further enhance the prototype's functionality. For instance, GPS could be used to provide location-based information, such as directions to a destination or alerts about upcoming landmarks. Smartphone apps could allow users to customize the feedback settings and access additional information about their surroundings.

While the ultrasonic glasses prototype is still in its early stages of development, it demonstrates the potential of innovative technologies to enhance spatial awareness for the visually impaired. By addressing the limitations and incorporating user feedback, future iterations of this prototype could become a valuable tool for promoting independence and safety for visually impaired individuals.

5. Emerging Technologies for Enhanced Spatial Awareness

As technology continues to evolve at a rapid pace, a plethora of new possibilities are emerging for enhancing spatial awareness in visually impaired individuals. These emerging technologies offer the potential to overcome the limitations of traditional assistive devices and universal design principles, providing more intuitive, personalized, and effective solutions.

5.1 Haptic Feedback Systems

Haptic feedback, the use of touch to communicate information, has emerged as a promising avenue for enhancing spatial awareness. Haptic feedback systems can provide directional cues, obstacle warnings, and environmental information through vibrations or other tactile sensations. This allows users to perceive spatial information without relying solely on auditory or visual cues.

One example of a haptic feedback system is the "Haptic Navigation Belt" developed by researchers at the University of Tokyo (Nagao et al., 2018). This belt uses a series of vibrating motors to provide directional cues to the wearer. The motors vibrate in different patterns to indicate the direction the user should move in, allowing them to navigate without having to constantly rely on a cane or guide dog.

Another promising application of haptic feedback is in the form of wearable devices like smart gloves or shoes. These devices can provide tactile feedback about the ground surface, helping users to detect changes in elevation, identify obstacles, and navigate complex terrains.

5.2 Augmented Reality (AR) and Virtual Reality (VR)

AR and VR technologies offer the potential to create immersive and interactive experiences that can significantly enhance spatial awareness for the visually impaired. AR overlays can provide real-time information about the user's surroundings, such as the names of objects, their distances, and directions to landmarks. This information can be presented visually, through text or images, or auditorily, through synthesized speech.

VR simulations can allow visually impaired individuals to virtually explore unfamiliar environments before physically navigating them. This can help users to build mental maps of their surroundings, familiarize themselves with landmarks and obstacles, and plan their routes in advance.

5.3 Smart Environments and the Internet of Things (IoT)

The concept of smart environments, where everyday objects are embedded with sensors and connected to the internet, holds great promise for enhancing spatial awareness for the visually impaired. Smart sensors can detect the presence of individuals and provide them with relevant information about their surroundings. For example, a smart door could announce its location and whether it is open or closed, while a smart shelf in a grocery store could provide audio descriptions of the products on display.

Furthermore, IoT devices can be used to control various aspects of the environment, such as lighting, temperature, and audio cues, to create a more accessible and comfortable experience for visually impaired individuals. For instance, smart lighting systems could automatically adjust to the user's preferences, while smart speakers could provide personalized audio guidance and information.

5.4 Artificial Intelligence (AI) and Machine Learning (ML)

AI and ML algorithms can play a crucial role in analyzing data from various sensors and providing personalized navigation assistance to visually impaired individuals. For example, AI-powered navigation systems could learn an individual's preferences and provide tailored directions based on their specific needs and abilities.

ML algorithms can also be used to develop more sophisticated object recognition systems, allowing visually impaired individuals to identify objects and landmarks in their environment with greater accuracy. This could significantly enhance their ability to navigate independently and interact with the world around them.

6. Towards a More Inclusive Future: Community-Based Approaches and Participatory Design

While technological advancements offer promising solutions, the development of truly inclusive spaces for the visually impaired necessitates a shift in focus towards community–based approaches and participatory design. It is essential to recognize that the visually impaired community possesses invaluable insights and lived experiences that can inform the design and implementation of effective solutions.

6.1 The Importance of User-Centered Design

User-centered design (UCD) is a design philosophy that places the needs, preferences, and limitations of end-users at the forefront of the design process. In the context of enhancing spatial awareness for the visually impaired, UCD involves actively involving visually impaired individuals in the design and evaluation of assistive technologies and environmental modifications.

By incorporating the perspectives of the visually impaired community, designers and researchers can gain a deeper understanding of the challenges faced by these individuals and develop solutions that are truly responsive to their needs. This collaborative approach can lead to the creation of more effective, user-friendly, and culturally relevant solutions.

6.2 Participatory Design and Co-creation

Participatory design (PD) takes the principles of UCD a step further by actively involving users in the co-creation of solutions. Through workshops, focus groups, and other collaborative activities, visually impaired individuals can share their experiences, insights, and preferences, contributing to the design process from its inception.

PD not only empowers the visually impaired community but also fosters a sense of ownership and agency over the solutions being developed. This can lead to greater adoption and acceptance of assistive technologies and environmental modifications, ultimately contributing to a more inclusive and accessible environment.

6.3 Real-World Examples of Community-Based Approaches

Several organizations and research initiatives have successfully employed community-based approaches to enhance spatial awareness for the visually impaired. For example, the Wayfindr project, a collaboration between the Royal National Institute of Blind People (RNIB) and ustwo, a digital product studio, developed a standardized system for audio wayfinding in public transportation environments. The project actively involved visually impaired individuals in the design and testing of the system, resulting in a solution that has been adopted by several transportation networks worldwide.

Another example is the Tactile Studio at the University of Dundee, which brings together researchers, designers, and visually impaired individuals to explore the potential of tactile and haptic feedback in enhancing spatial awareness. The studio's projects range from tactile maps and models to haptic navigation systems, all developed in close collaboration with the visually impaired community.

6.4 Challenges and Considerations

While community-based approaches and participatory design offer promising avenues for enhancing spatial awareness, several challenges and considerations need to be addressed. Ensuring meaningful participation of visually impaired individuals can be difficult, especially for those with limited mobility or communication barriers. Additionally, finding a balance between individual needs and preferences and the need for standardized solutions can be a challenge.

Despite these challenges, the benefits of community-based approaches far outweigh the drawbacks. By actively involving the visually impaired community in the design process, we can ensure that solutions are not only effective but also relevant, user-friendly, and culturally appropriate.

7. Conclusion

Enhancing spatial awareness for the visually impaired is a multifaceted challenge that necessitates a holistic approach. While existing assistive technologies and universal design principles have made strides in improving accessibility, there remain significant gaps and limitations that hinder the full participation of visually impaired individuals in society.

This research paper has highlighted the complexities of spatial awareness for this population, emphasizing the importance of understanding the unique challenges they face in perceiving and navigating their surroundings. The exploration of emerging technologies, such as haptic feedback, augmented reality, smart environments, and artificial intelligence, has revealed promising avenues for developing innovative solutions that could revolutionize spatial awareness and navigation.

The case study of the ultrasonic sensor-based glasses prototype, despite its limitations, serves as a testament to the potential of technology to augment existing assistive devices and provide real-time feedback about the environment. It also underscores the importance of user-centered design and the need to involve visually impaired individuals in the development and evaluation of new technologies.

Furthermore, the research emphasizes the importance of community-based approaches and participatory design in creating inclusive spaces. By engaging with the visually impaired community and incorporating their lived experiences and perspectives, designers and researchers can develop solutions that are not only effective but also relevant, user-friendly, and culturally appropriate.

As technology continues to evolve, we can expect to see even more innovative and sophisticated solutions emerge to enhance spatial awareness for the visually impaired. By embracing a multi-faceted approach that combines technology, universal design principles, and community engagement, we can create a future where visually impaired individuals can navigate their surroundings with confidence, independence, and dignity.

Future Directions

Future research should focus on:

- Further developing and refining emerging technologies like haptic feedback, AR, and smart environments to address the specific needs of visually impaired individuals.

- Conducting rigorous evaluations of these technologies in real-world settings to assess their effectiveness and usability.

- Exploring the potential of AI and ML algorithms to personalize navigation assistance and object recognition systems.

- Strengthening community-based approaches and participatory design to ensure that solutions are developed in collaboration with visually impaired individuals.

By investing in research and development, embracing emerging technologies, and fostering collaboration between researchers, designers, and the visually impaired community, we can create a world where spatial awareness is no longer a barrier to full participation in society for visually impaired individuals.

References

Blasch, B. B., Kurze, M., & Wallhoff, F. (2009). Technologies for the blind. In Springer

Handbook of Robotics (pp. 1277-1305). Springer. https://doi.org/10.1007/978-3-540-30301- 5-58

Golledge, R. G. (1997). Wayfinding behaviour: Cognitive mapping and other spatial processes. Johns Hopkins University Press.

Harper, S., & Shaw, C. (2017). Social isolation and loneliness among adults with visual impairment: A systematic review. British Journal of Visual Impairment, 35(3), 265-280.

Kim, Y., & Park, N. (2017). The effects of auditory cues on spatial awareness and navigation performance of visually impaired people. Journal of Visual Impairment & Blindness, 111(4), 381-394.

La Grow, S. J., & Weessies, K. (2016). The impact of visual impairment on mobility and independence. The Journal of Visual Impairment & Blindness, 110(1), 6-18.

Nagao, K., Amemiya, T., & Maeda, T. (2018). Haptic navigation belt: A wearable haptic device for directional navigation assistance. In Proceedings of the 2018 CHI Conference on

Human Factors in Computing Systems (pp. 1-11). https://doi.org/10.1145/3173574.3173746

Ungar, S. (2000). Cognitive mapping without visual input: What is the role of sonar? Journal of Visual Impairment & Blindness, 94(8), 465-477.

Wayfindr. (2023). Our story. Retrieved from https://wayfindr.net/

World Health Organization. (2019). World report on vision. Geneva: World Health Organization. https://www.who.mt/publications/i/item/world-report-on-vision

Acknowledgments

The authors would like to express their sincere gratitude to the visually impaired individuals from the Vividha Trust who generously participated in the prototype testing and provided invaluable feedback. Their insights and experiences were instrumental in shaping this research and guiding the development of potential solutions.

We also extend our appreciation to the physics and computer science departments at Headstart Educational Academy for their support and resources, which were crucial in the development and testing of the ultrasonic sensor-based glasses prototype.

Finally, we thank the numerous researchers, designers, and organizations whose work has contributed to the growing body of knowledge on enhancing spatial awareness for the visually impaired.

Appendix

A. Ultrasonic Sensor-Based Glasses Prototype: Technical Specifications and Design Schematics

This section provides a detailed overview of the ultrasonic sensor-based glasses prototype discussed in Section 5. It includes technical specifications of the components used, a schematic diagram illustrating the device's architecture, and a description of the algorithm used for distance calculation and auditory feedback generation.

A.1 Technical Specifications

Component	Specification
Ultrasonic Sensor	HC-SR04
Microcontroller	Arduino Uno
Buzzer	Piezoelectric buzzer
Power Supply	9V battery
Sensor Range	2cm - 400cm
Sensor Angle	15 degrees

Feedback Frequency   Variable (increasing with decreasing distance to object)

A.3 Algorithm Description

The algorithm used in the prototype is based on the principle of time-of-flight (TOF) measurement. The ultrasonic sensor emits a short burst of ultrasonic waves, which travel through the air and bounce off objects in the path. The sensor then measures the time taken for the reflected waves to return. By knowing the speed of sound in air, the distance to the object can be calculated using the following formula:

Distance = (Time of Flight * Speed of Sound) / 2

The calculated distance is then used to control the frequency of the buzzer's beeping sound.

As the distance to an object decreases, the frequency of the beeping increases, providing an auditory cue to the wearer about the proximity of obstacles. The specific frequency range and modulation can be adjusted to suit individual preferences and environmental conditions.

A.4 Limitations and Future Improvements

As discussed in Section 5, the prototype has several limitations, including the limited range of the sensor, the intrusiveness of the auditory feedback, and the lack of information about obstacles to the side or above. Future improvements could include:

- Using multiple sensors with a wider field of view to provide a more comprehensive understanding of the surroundings.

- Exploring alternative feedback mechanisms, such as haptic feedback through vibrations, to provide a more subtle and less intrusive form of communication.

- Integrating the sensor with other technologies, such as GPS and smartphone apps, to provide additional information and guidance.

- Developing machine learning algorithms to personalize the feedback and adapt to the user's specific needs and preferences.

Reference Images:

Enhancing Spatial Awareness: Object Tracking Glasses for Individuals with Visual Impairments

About the Authors:

Pavan Maiya

Pavan Maiya is a high-school student with a passion for hardware electronics, amassing over 10 years of hands-on experience in the field. His expertise extends to diverse projects pushing the boundaries of connected technologies, video processing, thermal reading, and architectural design. Pavan played a pivotal role in developing the foundational hardware and software components of the object-tracking glasses, contributing his extensive knowledge of hardware electronics to the project.

Email: *ppavanmaiya@gmail.com*

Pranav Bahven Savla

Pranav Bhaven Savla, also a high-school student, brings a wealth of experience in software development spanning 6 years. As the founder of the startup Phoenix Digital Media, Pranav has dedicated himself to empowering blind or visually impaired students to explore videography. Additionally, he co-founded Vidyadrishti, a non-profit organization focused on enhancing writing skills. Pranav is a two-time app developer with apps available on the Google Play Store and was recognized as the winner of the 2019 IStem Confluence and Hackathon. As a YouTuber, he shares his insights and knowledge with a global audience. In the object tracking glasses project, Pranav played a crucial role in developing the logical software, incorporating mathematical algorithms, contributing to the ergonomic design, and co-authoring this paper.

Email: *pranavsavla2003@gmail.com*

Daniel Marc Maani

With a background spanning one year in design, Daniel has brought his artistic expertise to the project, contributing to the formatting and visual presentation of this research paper.

Daniel's skills in crafting model kits, creating engaging videos, and capturing captivating photos have added a distinctive visual appeal to the documentation of our work. His keen eye for design and dedication to visual storytelling have played a vital role in ensuring the clarity and professionalism of this research paper.

Together, Pavan Maiya, Pranav Bhaven Savla, and Daniel Marc Maani represent a dynamic team with a diverse skill set that significantly contributed to the successful realization of the object-tracking glasses. Their combined expertise in hardware electronics, software development, entrepreneurship, and design underscores their commitment to innovation and accessibility in assistive technology.

Email: *thenightsfury911@gmail.com*

Overcoming Barriers: My Journey as a Student with Visual Impairment in STEM Education

Pranav Bhaven Savla
Software Engineering Student

As a student with visual impairment, my journey through STEM education—especially mathematics and science—has been both challenging and fulfilling. It has required creativity, determination, and a relentless desire to adapt to an environment not always designed with accessibility in mind. But over time, with the right tools, a supportive community, and unwavering resilience, I've been able to transform these challenges into opportunities. In this article, I will share my experiences, the obstacles I faced, and the solutions I developed, hoping to provide useful insights to others who may find themselves in a similar position.

The Initial Challenges: Navigating an Inaccessible World

When I first started my STEM education, the most immediate hurdle I faced was the lack of accessible learning materials. Mathematics, in particular, was a significant challenge. The visual nature of math equations, graphs, and geometric illustrations posed a severe obstacle. Science, with its complex diagrams, charts, and experimental setups, seemed equally daunting. In these fields, it often felt as if I was trying to learn a language that was foreign to me—one that was not built with my needs in mind.

One of the biggest frustrations was the absence of accessible math formatting and tools for students with visual impairments. In mathematics, for instance, the layout of equations in traditional textbooks, often in small font or with visual-only elements like graphs and illustrations, made them nearly impossible to comprehend without assistance. In many cases, even when I could access a text-to-speech tool or Braille format, the complex mathematical symbols and notations were not properly represented or were misinterpreted.

Science, too, presented similar issues. Experiments, which often rely on hands-on participation, require visual observation, but alternative approaches like tactile diagrams or audio descriptions are not always readily available. In fact, many educators themselves were unsure how to best adapt their methods to accommodate students with visual impairments.

Finding Solutions: The Power of Adaptation

I realized early on that I could not afford to wait for systems and processes to change for me. Instead, I had to take an active role in shaping my educational experience. A crucial step in my journey was discovering the importance of assistive technologies—tools that would level the playing field and make STEM subjects more accessible.

Math: The Power of Tactile Tools and Digital Solutions

For mathematics, I found that tactile solutions such as Braille math books, raised-line drawings, and tactile graphic organizers helped me understand the structure of equations, graphs, and diagrams. I used specialized devices like the BrailleNote, which allowed me to input equations using Braille, and a tactile graphics display to feel the layout of mathematical concepts. These tactile solutions gave me an intuitive understanding of abstract mathematical concepts that I had previously struggled with.

Additionally, digital tools such as MathSpeak and MathType provided text-to-speech solutions that read aloud mathematical symbols and equations. These tools often employed a system of describing each component of an equation, ensuring that I could follow along with the mathematical logic. However, while these tools were helpful, they were not without limitations. For instance, MathSpeak sometimes struggled to articulate more complex notations, and I had to rely on multiple resources to get a comprehensive understanding.

I also found that involving my teachers and peers in the process of learning mathematics was invaluable. With their help, I was able to understand how to approach mathematical problems in ways that didn't rely on visual input. Teachers who were willing to describe diagrams in vivid detail or walk me through problems step-by-step were essential to my success. This collaborative learning environment enabled me to tackle more difficult topics, like calculus and linear algebra, that I once thought were beyond my reach.

Science: Turning Complexity into Comprehension

In science, the real challenge was not just understanding the concepts but also participating in practical work and experiments. Many science concepts depend on physical demonstrations, and with visual impairment, this meant that I had to rely on descriptions from my teachers and fellow students. However, I was fortunate enough to be in an academic environment that recognized the importance of providing me with tactile or auditory materials.

For example, in physics, I used audio-based simulations to understand the principles of mechanics, motion, and energy. With the help of software like Audio Lab and interactive learning tools that described experiments, I could grasp scientific principles without being visually present. Additionally, tactile representations of molecular structures, chemical reactions, and anatomical models helped me visualize and interact with content that would otherwise be inaccessible.

I also found that discussing science concepts with other students, especially through group projects, allowed me to gain new insights and perspectives. Collaborative learning became a central part of my experience, where peers would assist in describing laboratory procedures, diagrams, and models. This enabled me to engage with science on a deeper level and brought a sense of inclusion that enhanced my learning experience.

The Importance of Advocacy and Support Systems

Another critical part of my journey in STEM was learning to advocate for myself. In the early stages, I wasn't sure how to approach my instructors and peers about my needs. However, I quickly realized that the key to overcoming challenges was communication. By expressing what I needed—whether it was audio descriptions, access to specific software, or the use of tactile diagrams—I found that teachers were more than willing to accommodate me.

Moreover, I sought out mentors—both in academia and the professional world—who were supportive and understood the unique challenges I faced. These mentors provided invaluable guidance on how to manage my time, stay motivated, and balance the rigorous demands of STEM education with my personal challenges.

Through this process, I learned that the importance of support systems cannot be overstated. For students with visual impairments, it is essential to have a network of people—teachers, mentors, peers, and organizations—that can offer encouragement and practical solutions. I also sought out communities of other blind students, which allowed me to share experiences and learn from others facing similar challenges. These support networks provided not only emotional reassurance but also concrete resources and advice for overcoming barriers.

Looking Ahead: The Future of STEM for Students with Visual Impairments

As I continue my studies and career in STEM, I remain optimistic about the future of accessibility in education. Technology is improving rapidly, and new tools are emerging every day that make STEM subjects more accessible to people with visual impairments. The advancements in AI, machine learning, and augmented reality hold great promise for creating more interactive and immersive learning experiences for students like me.

However, there is still much to be done. The education system must recognize the need for more widespread adoption of accessible tools and methods. Curriculum developers and educators must be trained to create materials that are inclusive of all students, regardless of their disabilities. In the long term, I hope to contribute to these efforts by advocating for improved accessibility standards and working towards creating a more inclusive STEM environment.

Conclusion: A Journey of Persistence and Resilience

My journey in STEM as a student with visual impairment has not been easy, but it has been incredibly rewarding. Each challenge I faced forced me to think outside the box, adapt, and find creative solutions. Along the way, I learned the importance of resilience, self-advocacy, and the power of collaboration. While the road has been difficult at times, it has also been a path of growth and empowerment.

To other students with visual impairments who may be reading this, I say: you are not alone. With the right tools, the right support, and a determination to succeed, there is no limit to what you can achieve in STEM. Embrace the challenges, find innovative solutions, and never forget that your perspective is unique and valuable in the world of science and technology.

To other students with visual impairments who may be reading this, I say: you are not alone. With the right tools, the right support, and a determination to succeed, there is no limit to what you can achieve in STEM. Embrace the challenges, find innovative solutions, and never forget that your perspective is unique and valuable in the world of science and technology.

Pranav Bhaven Savla
Bengaluru, Karnataka, India
Email: pranavsavla2003@gmail.com
Phone: +917022129798
linkedin.com/in/pranav-savla

A Forgotten Blind Mathematician Of India:
Story of Dr. Lakkoju Sanjeevarayalu,
22/11/1907 to 02/12/1997

Researched and written by:

Dr. G. S. Ramaiah

A mathematical genius born in the lesser-known village, Kallur, of the Proddatur constituency in Kadapa District, Andhra Pradesh, located on the banks of the Penna River. Although he is the pride of the district, he wasn't celebrated. One can try but not find a statue of him, recognizing his gifted talents as a mathematician. He is the first and the only mathematician in the world who has participated in over 6000 Ganitha Avadhanams (a mathematical show that uses Avadhanam—where an expert answers questions spontaneously and presents mathematical solutions) over 67 years.

Hailing from a family of Goldsmiths, born to Lakkoju Pedda Pullayya and Nagamamba, Sanjeevarayalu had Congenital Blindness. Back then, there were no organisations for the blind, nor was there the availability of Braille script in India. With no formal education, Sanjeevarayulu learned mathematics through his sister, who would loudly recite everything she learned from school at home. A single mother raised him (polygamy was prevalent in those periods). He used to earn a small sum by teaching the farmers in his village to measure the land and calculate the paddy yield rate. It was during this time that his passion for learning the violin began. He was a true patriot and a freedom fighter as well. He was married at the age of 19 to Adilakshmamma, and they have a son, Lakkoju Subbarayudu.

At the age of 20, in 1928, he performed in his first Ganitha Avadhanam, which continued up until 1995 covering over 6000 such mathematical shows. He participated in these Avadhanams for which he traveled to Andhra Pradesh, Karnataka, Maharashtra, Bihar and Delhi. He was a frequent visitor by invitation for many of the august gathering to show his Mathematical genius in metropolitan cities such as Delhi, Bengaluru, and Hyderabad. His performance was the main attraction in the Akhila Bharatiya Congress Mahasabha on 15/11/1928 in Nandiyal. During these Avadhanams, he would not only state the right answer but also give extensive details about these answers. For example, if the problem was a birth date, usually the answer would be on which day did that birth date fell in. But Sanjeevarayulu would also go into extensive detail about the astrology and the planetary movements of that day, on the spot. This extraordinary talent is so unique that no one to date has matched such precision and talent.

At one such event, in Hyderabad, he was asked what 2^{103} was, and he immediately gave a 32-digit answer. Many such instances were dealt with grace by Dr. Sanjeevarayulu. Such feet take a person more than an hour to derive an answer with pen and paper, to solve the complex mathematical problems that he solves within seconds, leaving everyone dumbstruck and in awe.

One of the most significant and notable instances was the chess incident. From the Sripada stories, the story of Vadla Ginjalu, or Grains, was asked, where the person who wins a game of Chess with the king would win grains. The winner then asked the number of grains where one square would have one grain, and it would double as the number of squares increased, totaling the number of squares to 64. There arose a question that, the sum of grains the winner would get, and Sanjeevarayulu easily solved this by stating that the winner would get 1, 84, 46, 74, 40, 73, 70, 95, 51, 615 grains. He also calculated the area covered by these grains, which is 20 times the distance between Earth and the Sun.

He has never seen numbers but has the capacity to calculate the most complex mathematical problems. He has created and gifted 4000-year calendars to the world. This gift of his was appreciated by various notable personalities such as Pandit Jawaharlal Nehru, Anne Besant, former President of India Dr. Rajendra Prasad, Beja Wada Gopala Reddy, Srimali, Humayun Kabir, Kasinadhuni Nageshwara Rao, P.V. Rajamannar, Governor Sir George Stanley, and the human-computer, the mathematical wizard Shakunatala Devi and many more. Babu Rajendra Prasad, the then President of India has also sanctioned 300 rupees as pension to Dr. Lakkoju Sanjeevarayalu.

He has performed before various universities and colleges, inspiring students. He has also performed in libraries and mathematical societies and was invited to the United States of America, but unfortunately, he could not attend the event due to visa problems. He was felicitated by various universities and presented gold medals. Unfortunately, on October 10, 1964, all his 14 gold medals were stolen on a train journey between Renigunta to Tirupati.

Unlike Sanjeevarayulu famous blind personalities such as John Milton, Louis Braille, Helen Keller, and Dwaram Venkataswamy Naidu were not blind by birth. We Indians recognize and honor famous mathematicians like Bhaskaracharya, Ramanujan, Shakuntala Devi, etc., who were all formally educated, whereas Dr. Lakkoju was not only blind but also never attended school. His only source of learning was through listening, and still, he is one of the world's top 6 greatest mathematicians.

The acting British viceroy (1934) and the then governor of Madras (1929-1934), George Stanley, once said that if Sanjeevarayulu were born in his country, Britain would honor him with a statue. Shakuntala Devi also appreciated him by stating that he was more talented than her. But he still lived his life in dire poverty. He was honored with an honorary doctorate by Sri Venkateshwara University. He received the Viswa Sankaracharya Award and the Anka Vidhyasagara Award. But his talent is beyond these prestigious awards, and it is immeasurable. He spent his last days at a Sathram (Shelter home) in Srikalahasti Temple, dedicating his time to playing the violin for the lord, for which he received 30 rupees per month as an honorarium.

This article brings this forgotten genius to light, hoping for him to be recognised just as well as other mathematicians are. This is a way of requesting a statue to be constructed in his honor in every state and also mentioning him as a part of history in textbooks. Just as Sir Ramanujam's birthday is celebrated as National Mathematics Day, the birthday of Dr. Lakkoju on November 22, should also be celebrated for his Chakshumathi Vidhya (intuitive mind) bound Mathematical powers, to make the world realize that to learn Mathematics, there is no need for eye or Braille or present-day digital tools for a blind. May be celebrated for the same. Because of the incapability of Braille and Mathematics, the world used to discourage such brilliant Chakshumathi minds from the blind community from learning mathematics in their schools.

Even though we have many such examples like Dr. T.V. Raman of Google, who was once denied his postgraduate studies in Mathematics by Indian Universities, which made him migrate to the United States of America and obtain a PhD in Mathematics and later teach mathematics at the Texas University. India lost Dr. Raman, just because the stories of Dr. Lakkoju were not widely spread and celebrated him as a national hero.

Dr. T.V. Raman is the architect of the new world order ruled by the Smartphone revolution. This senior research scientist of Google, who masterminded and started Accessibility as the core nature of Google, started with search engine optimization for all (blind and illiterates), the Android, Google Lens and now working on Google Translation to make our world a seamless one.

Raman developed screen reading technologies for his mathematical journeys by himself and he is the only Indian-origin computer scientist featured in a product at the Smithsonian Museum of Technology. His invention, Emacspeak is a free computer application, a speech interface, and an audio desktop (as opposed to a screen reader). He worked in IBM, Adobe Systems making PDF accessible, and now in Google changing the world to a new order with no disabilities.

Here we need to mention, two more blind prodigies in Mathematics. Bhavya Shaw, who just completed his degree in Mathematics at Stanford University in the United States, and the rise of another young mathematical genius Amman Ahamed, a first-standard student at the Indian School, Al Seeb Oman. At the age of 6, he does the pie of 200. They were brought up in the digital world built by Raman and most of the time they can use computing.

Dr. Lakkoju Sanjeevarayulu is a true inspiration not only to the blind but also to the young, energetic, and enthusiastic students and will forever be remembered as one. He needs to be celebrated by the world on his birthday like Louie Braille. If not, more able blind students will be denied to study Mathematics, Science, and Technology and have to migrate to new pasture fields.

About the author:

Dr. G. S. Ramaiah *was the alumina of Jawaharlal Nehru Technology University (JNTU), Anantapur, Andhra Pradesh, and after an illustrious career as a principal of Polytechnic Colleges, he retired as Inspector of Training. He is a Life Member of INTACH, Life Member of Andhra Pradesh History Congress, and the Patron of the Red Cross Society. He is now helping Andhra Pradesh to become Inclusive in education by consulting on Accessible Courses for Children with Special Needs (CwSN) to become professionals in emerging technologies in Project 2027 Inclusive Education, Andhra Pradesh.*

Understanding Individuals With Visual Impairment

"Kindness is the language which the deaf can hear and the blind can see"

Mark Twain

Sairabanu Daragad & Dr. Venkat Lakshmi. H.

Abstract

Individuals with visual impairments face unique challenges in their day to day lives, as they basically rely on alternative methods to navigate the world around them. Understanding and accommodating their needs is crucial in ensuring that they have equal access to opportunities and resources. These include providing augmentative and alternate communication and being mindful of physical barriers which may hinder their mobility. Understanding their concerns, supporting them to navigate and become independent is the need of the hour. This article provides an understanding about the prevalence, categories, identification, causes, features, and challenges faced by the visually impaired individuals.

It is important to create an inclusive environment for individuals with visual impairments which not only requires empathy but also proactive action. It involves recognizing the unique challenges they face and addressing them. By doing so, one can ensure that individuals with visual impairments have equal access to opportunities and resources in participating to fullest extent in the society. By embracing inclusivity, one can create more diverse and vibrant community that benefits everyone.

Introduction:

Vision impairment is an inability to correct a person's eyesight to a standard level, a condition that leads to a notable reduction in an individual's visual capabilities. This encompasses both partial and complete blindness, as well as conditions that affect the way visual information is perceived (Murthy, G., et.al, 2017). "Blindness" is characterized by a visual acuity worse than 20/400 with the best possible correction, or a visual field of 10 degrees or smaller(Mandal, Ananya., 2023). According to the World Health Organization, individuals with "low vision" have a visual acuity ranging from 20/70 to 20/400 with the best possible correction, or a visual field of 20 degrees or smaller (Centre for Disease Control, 2005). Various factors such as eye diseases, injuries, genetic conditions, and neurological disorders contribute to visual impairment. The extent of visual impairment can range from mild to severe, greatly affecting a person's ability to carry out daily activities. Nevertheless, with the aid of assistive technology and the support of medical experts, individuals with visual impairment can lead meaningful and autonomous lives (Dhayal, P., 2023).

Vision impairment is an inability to correct a person's eyesight to a standard level, a condition that leads to a notable reduction in an individual's visual capabilities. This encompasses both partial and complete blindness, as well as conditions that affect the way visual information is perceived (Murthy, G., et. al, 2017). "Blindness" is characterized by a visual acuity worse than 20/400 with the best possible correction, or a visual field of 10 degrees or smaller (Mandal, Ananya., 2023). According to the World Health Organization, individuals with "low vision" have a visual acuity ranging from 20/70 to 20/400 with the best possible correction, or a visual field of 20 degrees or smaller (Centre for Disease Control, 2005).Various factors such as eye diseases, injuries, genetic conditions, and neurological disorders contribute to visual impairment. The extent of visual impairment can range from mild to severe, greatly affecting a person's ability to carry out daily activities. Nevertheless, with the aid of assistive technology and the support of medical experts, individuals with visual impairment can lead meaningful and autonomous lives (Dhayal, P., 2023).

Prevalence: (WHO report 2023)

- At a global level, there are a minimum of 2.2 billion people who are facing challenges with their near or distance vision. In nearly half of these cases, which amount to 1 billion people, the vision impairment could have been prevented or remains unaddressed.

- Out of the total of 1 billion cases, the leading factors contributing to distance vision impairment or blindness are as follows: cataract affects 94 million individuals, refractive error affects 88.4 million individuals, age-related macular degeneration affects 8 million individuals, glaucoma affects 7.7 million individuals, and diabetic retinopathy affects 3.9 million individuals.

- Regional disparities show that the prevalence of distance vision impairment in low- and middle-income regions is approximately 4 times higher than in high-income regions. Over 80% of cases of near vision impairment remain unaddressed in Western, Eastern, and Central Sub-Saharan Africa, whereas rates in high-income regions like North America, Australia, Asia, Western Europe, and Asia-Pacific are below 10%.

- The risk of vision impairment is expected to rise due to population growth and aging.

Features of Visual Impairment (Targetb.ed, 2022)

Academic Characteristics

- For individuals who are completely blind, touch and auditory serve as a key source of information.

- For those who are partially blind, their vision is limited, making it difficult to see objects from a distance or read small print. They are largely dependent on large print materials.

- Both the totally and partially visually impaired rely profoundly on memory and auditory skills.

Physical Characteristics

- The motor skills of the visually impaired are often poor due to limited mobility.

- Despite having similar size and appearance to those with normal vision, their overall health may be slightly compromised due to mobility issues.

- Delayed development of locomotor behavior is also common among most of them.

Intellectual Characteristics

- It involves the formation of concepts.

- They rely on auditory or tactile learning to grasp information.

- As a result, most of the visually impaired individuals struggle with cognitive tasks as they lack observational experiences.

Behavioral Characteristics

- Visually impaired individuals often exhibit irritability due to maltreatment by others.

- Due which they may have low self-confidence, leading them to avoid social interactions.

- They are also impacted in the areas of social skills, emotional understanding, and non-verbal communication.

Communication Abilities

- Reading may be challenging for them.

- Communication skills may be poor during early stages of life, but tend to improve after the age of 18.

- They generally prefer oral communication over written communication, and may not enjoy reading or writing extensively.

Categories of Visual impairment

- Profoundly Impaired:Total blindness

- **Severely Impaired**: Partially sighted individuals with visual acuity below 6/60 even with the best possible correction.

- **Moderately Impaired**: Their impairment is not severe. They have visual acuity ranging from 6/24 to 6/60. With appropriate assistance, they can perform most of the daily living tasks.

- **Mildly Impaired**: Individuals with mild visual impairment do not experience any challenges performing their day-to-day tasks and have no limitations in their visual field.

Identification of Visual Impairment

Behavioral	Physical	Medical
<ul><li>Reports visual blurring.</li><li>Unable to sit for extended periods of reading or writing.</li><li>Lacks focus while doing cartography or while working on a blackboard work.</li></ul>	<ul><li>Persistent eye irritation or watery eyes, headaches.</li><li>Difficulty identifying finer details in pictures, blinking.</li><li>Struggles with reading small prints.</li></ul>	<ul><li>If the individuals can read only the letter on first line of the chart, their visual acuity is 6/60.</li><li>If they can read the second row of letters, their visual acuity is 6/36.</li><li>If they can read the second last line of the chart, their vision is considered normal, i.e., 6/6.</li></ul>

Causes: This can arise from various causes, such as genetic conditions, eye diseases, injuries, and neurological disorders(Global Burden of Disease Study, Lancet Glob Health. 2021).

- **Refractive Errors**: The most prevalent cause of vision loss is refractive errors, which occur when the shape of the eye hinders proper focusing of light on the retina. This can lead to blurry vision, near-sightedness, farsightedness, or astigmatism. Corrective measures for refractive errors often involve glasses, contact lenses, or refractive surgery.

- **Macular Degeneration**: is a condition that affects the macula, the central part of the retina, leading to vision loss. It is commonly associated with aging and can be categorized as either dry or wet macular degeneration. It impacts the macula, responsible for sharp central vision, and can result in the inability to read, recognize faces, or perform tasks requiring clear vision. Treatment options for macular degeneration may include medication, laser therapy, photodynamic therapy,or injections.

- **Glaucoma**: encompasses a group of eye diseases that damage the optic nerve, potentially leading to partial or complete vision loss. While it is often associated with high intra ocular pressure (IOP), it can also occur with normal IOP. Treatment for glaucoma may involve medication, laser therapy, or surgery.

- **Cataracts**: occur when the eye's lens becomes cloudy or opaque, resulting in blurred or dimmed vision. They are a common cause of vision loss in older adults and are frequently addressed through surgery to replace the affected lens with an artificial one.

- **Retinal Vein Occlusion**: is seen when a vein in the retina becomes blocked, leading to vision loss. It can be categorized as either branch retinal vein occlusion or central retinal vein occlusion. Treatment options for retinal vein occlusion may include medication, laser therapy, or injections.

- **Uveitis**: is an inflammation of the uvea, the middle layer of the eye, which can result in vision loss and other complications. It can be caused by various factors such as infection, autoimmune diseases, or trauma. Treatment for uveitis may involve medication, eye drops, or other therapies depending on the underlying cause.

Challenges faced by visually impaired

Visual impairment is a widespread condition affecting millions of individuals globally, stemming from various factors like genetics, illness, injury, or aging. The challenges faced by the visually impaired can hinder their daily activities and limit their involvement in social and economic endeavors. The impediments faced by the visually impaired and the available opportunities to assist them in overcoming these hurdles (Eyecan, 2023), are explained under the following:

Limited Accessibility: a major obstacle for the visually impaired is the restricted accessibility they encounter. This encompasses physical hindrances such as stairs, uneven surfaces, and the absence of handrails. Additionally, digital barriers like inaccessible websites, applications, and documents pose challenges.

Social Isolation: blurred vision can impede engagement in social activities, resulting in loneliness and isolation. Social isolation can also have adverse effects on mental health, including depression and anxiety. It is crucial to create avenues for the visually impaired to partake in social activities and establish connections with others.

Employment Opportunities: limited employment opportunities present another challenge for the visually impaired. Numerous jobs necessitate visual acuity or involve tasks that are challenging to execute without vision. This difficulty in finding meaningful employment and contributing to the workforce can be daunting.

Education: poses unique challenges for individuals with visual impairments. Traditional educational materials like textbooks and handouts are often inaccessible to them, hindering their ability to keep pace with their peers and excel academically. Fortunately, braille books, advancements in technology, such as screen readers and text-to-speech software, have made it easier for visually impaired students to access educational materials and achieve academic success.

Transportation: also presents obstacles for the visually impaired. Many modes of transportation, such as cars and bicycles, rely heavily on visual acuity and are not suitable for individuals with visual impairments. Additionally, public transportation can be challenging to navigate and may not be available in all areas. However, there are various assistive technologies designed to aid the visually impaired in transportation, including audible pedestrian signals and GPS navigation systems.

Devices for visually impaired

Individuals with visual impairment face unique challenges in their daily lives. Despite their visual limitations, they possess a wide range of practical skills that enable them to navigate and engage with the world around them.

One area where individuals with visual impairments excel is in adaptive technology. They can effectively use various assistive devices and software that enhance their independence and productivity. For example, they can proficiently operate screen readers, which convert text into speech or Braille, allowing them to access written information on computers or mobile devices. Additionally, they can utilize tactile maps and navigation systems to confidently move around unfamiliar environments.

Furthermore, individuals with visual impairment and practical abilities often develop exceptional spatial awareness and memory skills. They can mentally map out their surroundings, memorize routes, and navigate through complex spaces with ease. This ability extends beyond physical spaces and applied to organizing or locating objects in their homes or workspaces.

In terms of employment, individuals with visual impairment can excel in a wide range of professions. Many have developed strong problem-solving and critical thinking skills, which are highly valued in fields such as engineering, computer programming, and scientific research.

Moreover, individuals with visual impairment often possess excellent communication and interpersonal skills. They practice the art of communicating their needs and preferences effectively, as well as advocate for themselves in various social and professional settings. Their ability to adapt and collaborate with others makes them a valuable team member and leader.

Further they can be supported in developing functional skills to perform their everyday tasks and activities. These abilities can include skills such as walking, standing, lifting, carrying, problem-solving, decision-making, and emotional regulation. Maintaining and improving functional abilities is essential for overall well-being and independence. Physical therapy, occupational therapy, and other interventions can aid in enhancing their functional abilities and maintain a high quality of life.

Age appropriateness is crucial while providing instruction. To cater to older students, using authentic materials is a great way to ensure age appropriateness. For instance, it would not be suitable to give a

13-year-old student an infant/toddler toy to entertain themselves, even if they are functioning at a much younger developmental level. Additionally, when developing lesson plan, it is essential to consider the individual needs, the objectives and plan IEP goals accordingly.

When teaching skills to individuals with visual impairment, it is important to use the natural and familiar environments or settings as it allows them to anticipate activities in a more natural way. It is crucial to teach skills within the environments to help them develop resilience.

To support them with cognitive disabilities, it is recommended to provide simple and clear verbal directions. Breaking tasks down into smaller parts that can be easily accomplished is also helpful. Simplifying tasks by reducing the number of steps, using techniques such as backward chaining and spiraling, can further support their learning.

It is essential for all individuals to develop their **literacy skills**, as a mandate and teachers must provide instructions for all. The "No Child Left behind Act" requires that all individuals/ students receive this instruction throughout their academic journey.

Conclusion:

Vision loss refers to the partial or complete inability to see, resulting in a decrease in visual acuity or clarity. This can be caused by a variety of factors, including eye diseases such as glaucoma, macular degeneration, diabetic retinopathy, and cataracts, as well as conditions like retinal detachment, optic nerve damage, and stroke. Vision loss can be temporary or permanent, and can greatly impact a person's quality of life, independence, and ability to perform daily tasks. Treatment options for vision loss vary depending on the underlying cause, and may include corrective lenses, medication, surgery, or vision rehabilitation therapy.

Visual impairment poses numerous challenges for both individuals and society. Nevertheless, there exist numerous avenues to assist the visually impaired in overcoming these obstacles and leading enriching lives. Through emphasizing accessibility, fostering social interactions, broadening job prospects, offering inclusive education, and enhancing transportation choices, we can facilitate the full integration of the visually impaired into society.

In conclusion, individuals with visual impairments possess a unique set of skills and strengths that enable them to overcome challenges and thrive in various aspects of life. Their proficiency in adaptive technology, spatial awareness, problem-solving, and communication make them valuable contributors to society and demonstrate the importance of inclusivity and accessibility for all individuals.

References:

Books:

1. Batshaw, M.L., (1997). Children with disabilities (4th edition). Baltimore, MD: Paul H. Brookes Publishing Co.

2. Carmen, Willings., (2017). Teachingvisuallyimpaired.com.

3. Day, S., (1997). Normal and abnormal visual development. In: Taylor D, editor. Paediatric Ophthalmology (2nd edition). Malden, MA: Blackwell Science; p 13-28.

4. Gudlavalleti, V.S. Murthy., and Neena, S. John., (2017). Chapter 13 - Public Health Eye Care: Modeling

Techniques to Translate Evidence Into Effective Action, Editor(s): Arni, S.R., Srinivasa, Rao., Saumyadipta, Pyne., C, R. Rao., Handbook of Statistics, Elsevier, Volume 37, Pages 317-345, https://doi.org/10.1016/bs.host.2017.09.006.

5. Holbrook, M.C., (Editor) (1996). Children with visual impairments: a parents' guide. Bethesda, MD: Woodbine House.

6. Kaminer, R.K., McMahon, E., (1995). Blindness and visual impairment. Pediatrics in Review; 16:77-8.

7. Mandal, Ananya., (2023). Types of visual impairment. https://www.news-medical.net/health/Types-of-visual-impairment.aspx.

8. Preetam, Dhayal., (2023). Special Education. https://www.specialeducationnotes.in/2023/03/what-is-visual-impairment-vi.html.

9. Puckett, C.D., (2001). The educational annotation of ICD-9-CM (4th edition). Reno, NV: Channel Publishing, Ltd., p. 641.

10. Sonksen, P.M., Petrie, A., and Drew, K.J., (2004). Promotion of visual development of severely visually impaired babies: evaluation of a developmentally based program. Developmental Medicine and Child Neurology 1991; 33:320-35. Date: October 29, 2004 Content source: National Center on Birth Defects and Developmental Disabilities.

11. Wang, C.W., (2014). Overview of Quality of Life Research in Older People with Visual Impairment.

Website:

https://eyecanofficial.medium.com/the-problems-faced-by-the-visually-impaired-understanding-the-challenges-and-opportunities-d20fc367c036

https://targetb-ed.co.in/visual-impairment/

https://www.who.int/news-room/fact-sheets/detail/blindness-and-visual-impairment

https://www.specialeducationnotes.in/2023/04/paper-1-introduction-to-disability-unit_61.html

https://www.teachingvisuallyimpaired.com/functional-skills.html

https://www.njstatelib.org/what-is-visual-impairment/

About authors:

Dr. Venkat Lakshmi. H, *is a Professor and HOD at the Department of Human Development, Smt. VHD Central Institute of Home Science, Maharani Cluster University, Bangalore. Her areas of expertise include early childhood education, special education, counseling, life skill education and welfare programs. Dr. Venkat Lakshmi. H has made significant contributions to her field through numerous publications in journals and books. She actively engages in research and provides guidance for M.Sc. and Ph.D. students in the aforementioned areas. Throughout her career, she has focused on special education issues, which she incorporates into her classroom teaching to empower each student and promote a life of dignity.*

Email Id: *anju.venks@gmail.com*

Dr. Sairabanu Daragad has been serving as a Guest Faculty in the Department of Human Development since 2019 in a temporary capacity. Previously, she held the position of Research Associate on a temporary basis at the University of Agricultural Sciences, Dharwad, Karnataka. She earned her Ph.D. degree from Bangalore University in 2019 and was also granted the MANF fellowship for her Doctoral Research work from 2016 to 2019. With 6 years of teaching experience at the Department of Human Development, School of Home Science, Maharani Cluster University Bangalore, and 3 years of experience in research projects. Dr. Daragad has made significant contributions to her field. She has published 20 research articles in UGC approved National and International journals, as well as presented research papers at 15 National and International conferences. Additionally, she has authored two books and received two awards for her conference presentations. Dr. Daragad has been honored with the Young Scientist Award and has published three standardized scales.

Email Id- d.*sairabanu@gmail.com*

Towards Financial Inclusion for Persons with Visual Impairment:

Addressing Ableism to Pave the Way for Barrier-Free Access to Banking and Other Financial Services

Dr. Sam Taraporevala
Executive Director- XRCVC,

Ketan Kothari
Managing Consultant – Programs, XRCVC,

Disha Kapadia-Chinchwadkar
Lead Consultant – Awareness (Advocacy), XRCVC (Xavier's Resource Centre for the Visually Challenged, St. Xavier's College, Mumbai)

Abstract

As the Republic of India celebrates its 75th year as a sovereign socialist state, its Constitution guarantees its citizens certain fundamental rights including the Rights to Equality and Freedom. It lays down Directive Principles for State Policy to protect the rights of marginalized communities to enable their inclusion in society.

An important aspect of inclusion is financial inclusion. Barrier-free sustainable access to financial services like banking, credit, savings, investments, insurance etc enhances inclusion of persons with visual impairment in mainstream society and benefits the economy.

Historically, persons with visual impairment were considered at par with illiterate persons for availing banking services. With India's ratification of the UNCRPD (2008), the concurrent awareness and advocacy work of the XRCVC, St. Xavier's College, Mumbai with the RBI and the Indian Banks Association, the RPwD Act (2016) and the BIS' IS -17802, comprehensive policy has been drafted to ensure financial services such as banking are made accessible for persons with visual impairment. Furthermore, the Government of India has recently notified of a draft of Rights of Persons with Disabilities (Amendment) Rules, 2024 for accessibility standards and guidelines for Banking Sector providing actionable steps to implement the legal and regulatory mandate.

The picture on-ground is bleak. Despite legal and regulatory mandate, there is a denial of basic banking services to persons with visual impairment, lack of accessibility in information and communication infrastructure creating exclusion from digital services like digital banking, entrenched ableism and lack of awareness among stakeholders and lack of financial literacy among persons with visual impairment.

This can be addressed through government initiatives and special drives, comprehensive policy formulation, compliance audits on accessibility, and awareness and training programs. These can be taken up through collaborations with various stakeholders for policy formulation and implementation.

Key words: Banking, Financial Inclusion. Accessibility, Inclusion

1. Introduction

The Republic of India celebrated its 75th year as a sovereign socialist state this year. Its Constitution guarantees all citizens certain fundamental rights including the Right to Equality and the Right to Freedom. Financial inclusion of marginalized communities plays an important role in their inclusion in society and enjoyment of these rights. It has been one of the key focus areas of government policy in recent years. However, the financial inclusion of persons with disabilities (PWDs) has not been a priority item for this policy.

This paper primarily analyses the ground-level reality of inclusion in banking services for persons with visual impairment (VI) as the major thrust of legal and regulatory mandates is on these services. However, the learnings from the creation of access in banking services for persons with VI can be applied to work towards financial inclusion for persons with VI in other financial services.

2. Background of Financial Inclusion for Persons with Visual Impairment in India

Historically, there were no regulations or provisions for persons with VI to independently access banking and other financial services and they were considered at par with illiterate persons for these services. Entrenched ableist attitudes, lack of awareness and sensitisation about the lives of persons with disabilities and lack of optimum use of technology kept financial and economic independence out of the reach of persons with VI, even though they were gainfully employed.

In 2005, the Court of the Chief Commissioner of Persons with Disabilities (CCPD) in the Case No. 2791 of 2003 in the case of V.P Singhania vs Banking Division, Ministry of Finance, Government of India, Indian Banks' Association (IBA) and the Reserve Bank of India (RBI) passed on order that stated that persons with VI should be allowed to open accounts and issued cheque books upon giving an undertaking and avail other services such as lockers without joint account and cash withdrawal with assistance of bank officials and that ATMs are accessible to all PWD users.

The Xavier's Resource Centre for the Visually Challenged, St. Xavier's College, Mumbai (XRCVC) set out to further address this lack of access for persons with VI in mainstream banking through its financial access initiative to ensure equitable rules and regulations for access to financial services. From 2006, XRCVC knocked on the doors of regulators such as Reserve Bank of India (RBI) and the National Securities Depository Ltd (NSDL) to create awareness and champion the rights of persons with VI. XRCVC's awareness, advocacy and consultancy work with regulators and policy makers such as the RBI, the Indian Bank's Association (IBA) and the NSDL successfully brought about changes in policy from 2008 onwards that created access for persons with VI in mainstream financial services and made provisions for them to independently open and operate bank and demat accounts on the principle of their competency to contract.

3. Legal and Regulatory Mandate on Financial Inclusion for Persons with VI

3.1 Legal Mandate

3.1.1. Rights of Persons with Disabilities Act (2016) and Rights of Persons with Disabilities Rules (2017)

India's ratification the United Nations Convention on the Rights of Persons with Disabilities (UNCRPD) led to the enactment of the Rights of Persons with Disabilities Act (2016). The RPWD Act protects and promotes various rights of persons with disabilities, including economic and financial. This Act lays down mandates and timelines applicable to all establishments and organisations – government, non-government and private to ensure accessibility of infrastructure and services.

The Rights of Persons with Disabilities (RPWD) Act Rules, notified in 2017 primarily focus on enhancing inclusivity and accessibility for persons with disabilities in India Most importantly, these provide specific inputs and timelines for ensuring reasonable accommodations and promoting barrier-free environments in both physical and Information and Communication Technology (ICT) infrastructure in public and private services ensuring integration of persons with disabilities in society.

On 2nd February, 2024 the Department of Financial Services, Ministry of Finance, Government of India notified "Accessibility Standards and Guidelines for Banking Sector" with intent to address accessibility needs of PwDs with respect to the facilities and services of the Banking Sector, in consultation with stakeholders and office of the CCPD. These provide guidelines for accessibility of physical infrastructure, ICT infrastructure, training and awareness for bank employees and other steps to ensure banking services are extended barrier-free to PwDs including VI.

In 2024, the Department of Empowerment of Persons with Disabilities (DEPWD) published a notice inviting public comments on the Draft of Rights of Persons with Disabilities (Amendment) Rules, 2024 on Sector wise Standards/Guidelines for Accessibility standards and guidelines for Banking Sector by Department of Financial Service. These drafted Rules outline in detail specific accessibility standards and guidelines for the banking sector under different heads such as physical infrastructure accessibility, accessibility of ICT, accessible communication, digital documents, and training and awareness for bank staff and other steps to facilitate banking services for PWDs including VI.

3.1.2. Bureau of Indian Standards' IS 17802 Parts 1 and 2

The Bureau of Indian Standards (BIS)' IS 17802 Parts 1 and 2 ensure a "cohesive, consistent and cross-cutting standard on accessibility requirement for ICT products and services used in all sectors" (Bureau of Indian Standards) and has dedicated guidelines for all ICTs as per categories such as stationary ICT, web, mobile and embedded software and non-web documents.

3.2. Regulatory Mandate

3.2.1. Reserve Bank of India Notifications

The RBI under the powers conferred upon it by the Banking Regulation Act (1949) section 35A has issued several notifications and circulars directing banks to ensure person with VI have equitable access to banking services. The key points of these are summarised below:

- The RBI notification dated 4th June, 2008, paved the way for barrier free access by directing that banking facilities including cheque book facility / operation of ATM / locker etc. cannot be denied to the VI as they are legally competent to contract.

- The RBI Notification dated 5th September, 2012 asked banks to ensure accessibility of internet banking services provided by them for persons with VI.

- The RBI directed banks to make all new ATMs accessible talking ATMs with Braille keypads and develop a road map for converting existing ATMs in its notification dated 11th June, 2015. Banks were directed to review this from time to time.

- The RBI Master Circular dated 1st July 2015 laid down Customer Services guidelines for persons with disabilities emphasizing on the areas of making bank branches and ATMs accessible for persons with disabilities through relevant physical infrastructure, providing all banking facilities to persons with VI and ensuring relevant assistance and implementation of talking ATMs with Braille keypads for persons with VI.

- The RBI Ombudsman scheme of 2021 is a redressal mechanism for persons with VI to barrier-free access to financial services provided by the entities identified under this scheme.

- The RBI issued a communication to all public sector, private sector and foreign banks dated 22nd February, 2024 in light of its incognito visits to branches of banks highlighting violations of norms laid down for accessible banking directing them to ensure compliance of said norms and furnish relevant records.

3.2.2. Indian Banks' Association Guidelines

The IBA worked closely with the XRCVC to develop appropriate guidelines and standards for accessibility of banking services which include:

- The IBA issued guidelines dated 18th November, 2008, directing all banks to provide persons with VI all banking facilities and further suggested harnessing developments in fingerprint technology to extend cheque book facility to a larger segment of persons with VI.

- The "Standards of Accessible ATMs" adopted by the IBA on 27th February, 2013 laid down accessibility features and process standards for ATMs to ensure persons with blindness and low vision and wheelchair users can independently access and operate these facilities.

- The IBA Circular dated 16th January, 2014 referred to the directives of the RBI to make banking services accessible to persons with VI and the challenges faced by them on ground in accessing these facilities. It also refers to the "Standards of Accessible ATMs" that can be used as a comprehensive guide to ensure accessibility of ATM services. It also directs banks to display posters outside accessible ATMs for persons with low vision.

- IBA Notification dated 5th February, 2015 on Model Customer Rights Policy based on the RBI Draft Charter of Customer Rights recognises 5 basic customer rights that are integral to financial inclusion for marginalised sections including persons with visual impairment.

- The IBA laid down a model policy for grievance redressal in banks based on principles of fair treatment to customers at all times, courteous and timely response to complaints, providing information to customers regarding avenues to escalate complaints and right to alternative remedy to protect their rights and the reputation of the bank.

- The IBA also published a report by the Working Group of IBA on Banking Facilities for Persons with Special Needs dated 4th June, 2018 that focused on four key areas – overall accessibility, physical accessibility of branches, accessibility of credit and accessibility in use of technology, websites, apps etc.

3.3. Illustrative Case Law

3.3.1 CCPD Order Dated 23.02.2012

This order issued in the case of Ramji Tripathi vs State Bank of India Banaras Hindu University Branch upheld the rights of persons with VI to equal access to all banking facilities and safety measures should not compromise these rights requiring them to submit additional undertakings etc.

3.3.2. High Court of Delhi Order dated 29.07.2022

The High Court of Delhi issued this order in the ongoing case of WP(C) 694/2020 of Mr. George Abraham vs Union of India and others along with several other public interest petitions clubbed with this lead case. A seven-member High Powered Committee of experts was constituted to look into the difficulties being faced by persons with VI in accessing financial services and to recommend practical applicable solutions. The said Committee has worked on an extensive report regarding accessible banking for various stakeholders and the matter is currently sub-judice.

4. Ground-Level Reality

While there is strong legal and regulatory mandate that gives access to financial services, particularly banking, to persons with visual impairment and enables their financial inclusion through relevant accommodations and accessibility standards and guidelines, the ground-level reality is starkly different that the picture imagined by the legal and regulatory mandate. Some of the key issues include:

4.1. Denial of banking services to persons with VI

There are many instances of denial of banking services reported even today despite the legal and regulatory mandate creating access to all banking facilities for persons with VI since 2008. The XRCVC in its 2022 report "Banking on Accessibility - A case for accessible banking for Persons with Disabilities (PwDs)" collated cases on denial of banking services as reported in different forums including the Eyeway Helpdesk Some common themes of these included:

- Denial of credit – either through loans or credit cards

- Signature issues

- Denial of cheque book, ATM cards,

- Requiring witnesses to open a bank account

- Requirement of undertakings for availing facilities

- Inaccessibility of ICT amounting to denial of digital banking services

Lack of awareness about the rules and regulations, entrenched ableist attitudes, assumption of illiteracy, assumption of persons with VI not being productively engaged in economic activity primarily underlie this. Moreover, financial services such as credit, savings, investments, insurance have higher barriers to access for PWDs including VI due to internal policies of banks that are not disability-friendly.

4.2. Lack of Accessibility of Information and Communication Technology

Banking and other financial services-related ICT infrastructure is highly inaccessible for persons with VI as there is a major gap in the implementation of accessibility standards set out.

The XRCVC conducted a study on the accessibility of ICT of the banking sector for persons with VI reported in "Banking on Accessibility: A case for accessible banking for Persons with Disabilities (PWDs)" in 2022. This study found that most major bank's websites, apps, online documents faired poorly on preliminary tests on basic accessibility parameters.

Some key highlights of the findings of this study are:

4.2.1. Banking Websites

This study did a preliminary test of the websites of 11 public sector banks, 6 private sector banks and 5 foreign banks and it was found that:

Table 1: Test Summary of Bank Websites

Testing Elements	Number of Public Sector Bank Websites (11)			Number of Private Sector Bank Websites (6)			Number of Foreign Bank Websites (5)			Total Passed on (22)
	Passed	Failed	Not Found/ NA	Passed	Failed	Not Found/ NA	Passed	Failed	Not Found/ NA	
Keyboard Operable	6	5	NA	3	3	NA	2	3	NA	11
Form Elements	2	9	NA	0	6	NA	3	2	NA	5
Captcha	1	9	1	1	4	1	0	0	5	2
Descriptive link (Read More, Click Here)	0	11	NA	0	6	NA	3	2	NA	3
Focus visibility	6	5	NA	1	5	NA	4	1	NA	11
Zooming	11	0	NA	6	0	NA	5	0	NA	22
Colour Contrast	1	10	NA	0	6	NA	3	2	NA	4
Accessibility Statement/ Features	10	1	NA	2	4	NA	4	1	NA	16

Source: *Banking on Accessibility: A case for accessible banking for Persons with Disabilities (PwDs), XRCVC, St. Xavier's College, Mumbai, Page 2*

4.2.2. Banking Apps

The XRCVC in this study also did basic accessibility tests of the android apps of 11 public sector banks, 6 private sector apps and 5 foreign banks. Here it was found that:

Table 2: Test Summary of Banking Apps

Testing Elements	Number of Public Sector Bank Apps (11)			Number of Private Sector Bank Apps (6)			Number of Foreign Bank Apps (5)			Total Passed on (22)
	Passed	Failed	Not Found/ NA	Passed	Failed	Not Found/ NA	Passed	Failed	Not Found/ NA	
Keyboard / Gesture Operable	11	0	NA	4	2	NA	4	1	NA	19
Form Elements	2	9	NA	0	6	NA	1	4	NA	3
Captcha	1	1	9	0	0	6	0	0	5	1
Descriptive link (Read More, Click Here)	0	11	NA	0	6	NA	2	3	NA	2
Focus visibility	10	1	NA	4	2	NA	4	1	NA	18
Zooming	11	0	NA	6	0	NA	5	0	NA	22
Colour Contrast	2	9	NA	0	6	NA	2	3	NA	4
Touch Target Size	0	11	NA	0	6	NA	0	5	NA	0

Source: *Banking on Accessibility: A case for accessible banking for Persons with Disabilities (PwDs), XRCVC, St. Xavier's College, Mumbai, Page 3*

4.2.3. Accessibility of Online Documents on Banks Corporate Websites

The XRCVC in the above study also found that none of the banks have properly tagged fully accessible PDF documents. PDFs that were passable were mostly searchable ones or HTML pages. Thus, banks do not seem to be aware of nor have implemented best practices on online document accessibility.

4.2.4. Lack of Accessible ATMs

Despite the legal mandate of the RPWD Act (2016) and RPWD Rules (2017), the regulatory guidelines laid down by RBI that all ATMs from 2014 onwards be talking accessible ATMs and the guidelines laid down by the Indian Banks' Association in their Standards for Accessible ATMs, there has been very little action on ground to implement these. Currently, there is no updated data on the accessible ATMs by banks provided post 2019. Moreover, most ATMs marked as "Talking ATMs" have only very basic audio feedback and not the entire process as mandated by the guidelines. Furthermore, accessibility is still not a part of the culture of banks, thus excluding persons with visual impairment from newly developed services such as UPI-enabled cash withdrawal.

4.2.5. Accessibility of Third-Party Wallets and UPI Apps

Table 3: Test Summary of Third-Party Wallets and UPI Apps

Number of Wallets and UPI Apps: 6

Testing Elements	Passed	Failed	Not Found/NA	Total Passed on (6)
Keyboard / Gesture Operable	6	0	NA	6
Form Elements	1	5	NA	1
Captcha	NA	NA	6	NA
Descriptive link (Read More, Click Here)	1	5	NA	1
Focus visibility	6	0	NA	6
Zooming	6	0	NA	6
Colour Contrast	2	4	NA	2
Touch Target Size	2	4	NA	2

Source: *Banking on Accessibility: A case for accessible banking for Persons with Disabilities (PwDs), XRCVC, St. Xavier's College, Mumbai, Page 4*

4.3. Lack of Awareness and Training

The root cause of barriers to banking and financial services access for persons with VI is a lack of awareness and appropriate training of bank staff and lack of awareness among persons with VI about their rights.

4.3.1. Bank Employees

Most banking staff from leadership to frontline branch staff in a majority of banks are still unaware of the legal and regulatory mandate and provisions, accessibility standards etc for providing banking services to persons with VI. Even if they are aware, they are not appropriately equipped with skills or tools to ensure all banking services are made adequately accessible for persons with VI leading to further exclusion from these services.

4.3.2. Persons with VI

Persons with visual impairment themselves are not aware of most of the provisions for banking access for them or the grievance redressal mechanisms available to them on denial of banking services.

4.4. Lack of Appropriate Grievance Redressal Mechanisms

While the RBI Ombudsman Scheme covers all banking customers, including VI, however banks are not well-equipped to support and address the grievances raised by PWDs including VI. Some of the key reasons grievances raised by PWDs, including VI, are not appropriately addressed include: lack of awareness of rules and regulations among bank staff, lack of awareness about accessibility needs, lack of training about Assistive Technology for providing appropriate support etc.

5. The Way Ahead

The problem of financial inclusion of persons with VI despite legal and regulatory mandates is multi-fold and thus needs to be addressed holistically. Some recommendations to ensure effective financial inclusion for the VI community include:

- Comprehensive policy formulation by the government and relevant regulators with a focus on **appropriate penalties for non-conformation** to these policies. This is currently lacking in the policy set out, leading to non-compliance as it is not a priority.

- Regulators to have regular **monitoring mechanisms** for financial inclusion for persons with VI such as accessibility audits, reports on implementation of accessible physical and ICT infrastructure, reports on complaints raised by persons with VI and their redressal etc. to protect their customer rights.

- Regulators such as the RBI or NSDL can set up an exclusive **Accessibility cell or a centre of excellence** for PwDs, including VI that monitors provisions for financial services to them, development of inclusive financial products that meet their needs, monitors accessibility of financial services infrastructure to ensure needs of PwDs are adequately met.

- Providing **awareness programs and training to bank leadership and staff** on lives of persons with VI, regulatory mandates, meeting their needs as customers, Assistive Technology, accessible content creation etc to equip them with the right tools.

- **Financial Literacy programs** targeted for persons with VI that educates them about financial services they can avail and special provisions for them, their customer rights, grievance redressal mechanisms available to them such as the RBI Ombudsman Scheme (2021).

- The government along with other policy makers and relevant stakeholders

- The government and regulatory authorities can address design, implementation and skill gaps by **partnering with stakeholders** such as not for profits with specialized skill set required to build accessibility into the system, vendors for development of specialized accessible infrastructure and technology etc.

- The issue of funding of financial inclusion measures can be done through private funding, CSR funding for implementation of awareness and training programs, accessing underutilized funds under SIPDA as appropriate.

6. Concluding Thoughts

Financial inclusion plays a key role in inclusion of marginalized communities in mainstream society. Barrier-free sustainable access to financial services like banking, credit, savings, investments, insurance etc opens up avenues of opportunities for the inclusion of historically marginalized communities such as persons with visual impairment in society and economy, ensuring their "full and effective participation in society" and innumerable benefits to the economy at large.

References

Bureau of Indian Standards. BIS IS 17802 (Part 1) : 2021: Accessibility for the ICT Products and Services - Part 1 Requirements. 2021, broadbandindiaforum.in/wp-content/uploads/2022/08/IS-17802_1_2021.pdf Accessed 10 Mar. 2024.

BIS IS 17802 Part (2) : 2022: Accessibility for the ICT Products and Services - Part 2 Determination of Conformance. 2022, broadbandindiaforum.in/wp-content/uploads/2022/08/IS-17802_2_2022.pdf. Accessed 10 Mar. 2024.

Department of Finance, Ministry of Financial Services, Government of India. Accessibility Standards and Guidelines for Banking Sector. 2 Feb. 2024.

Government of India. "The Rights of Persons with Disabilities Act." Office of Chief Commissioner for Persons With Disabilities, DEPwD, MSJE, Government of India, 2016, www.ccdisabilities.nic.in/actsguideline/disability-acts.

Indian Banks' Association. "Standards for Accessible ATM Adopted by Indian Banks' Association." Talking ATM India, 2013, talkingatmindia.org/Download.aspx?name=IBA%20standards%20on%20Accessible%20ATM_27February2013.pdf. Accessed 20 May 2024.

Sharma, Satish Chandra, CJ, and Subramonium Prasad J. "Order 29.07.2022 CM APPL. 18601/2022 in W.P.(C) 694/2020 In the High Court of Delhi at New Delhi." Delhi High Court Order Information System, 29 July 2022, dhcappl.nic.in/dhcorderportal. Accessed 22 May 2024.

Xavier's Resource Centre for the Visually Challenged (XRCVC). "Accessible ATMs in India – a Retrospective and Prospective View - a Case for Enhancing Accessibility of ATMs for Persons With Visual Impairment." The Xavier's Resource Centre for the Visually Challenged, 2024, xrcvc.org/docs/XRCVC_ATM_Accessibility_Paper.pdf. Accessed 20 May 2024.

"Bankers Guide to Inclusive Banking." The Xavier's Resource Centre for the Visually Challenged, 2013, xrcvc.org/docs/bankers-guide-to-inclusive-banking.pdf. Accessed 21 May 2024.

"Banking on Accessibility: A case for accessible banking for Persons with Disabilities (PWDs)." The Xavier's Resource Centre for the Visually Challenged, 2022, xrcvc.org/docs/Banking%20on%20Accessibility%20by%20XRCVC%20June%202022.pdf. Accessed 20 Mar. 2024.

Author Bios

Dr. Sam Taraporevala *is the founder of XRCVC, St. Xavier's College, Mumbai and currently is its Executive Director. Dr. Sam is a Sociology academician and also a renowned name in the field of disability. He has been a part of several academic committees and National Disability bodies including Member, Board of Studies, Department of Sociology and Anthropology and Member, Internal Quality Assurance Cell (IQAC), St. Xavier's College, Mumbai; Member, Braille Council of India; Member, General Council, National Institute for the Visually Handicapped (NIVH), Dehradun and Vice President & Chair, Committee on Policy Intervention & Higher Education, DAISY Forum of India, to name a few. He retired in 2019 as Associate Professor and the Head of Department of Sociology at St. Xavier's College, Mumbai.*

Ketan Kothari: *With over 30 years of experience in the field of disability, Ketan's role at the XRCVC involves end-to-end implementation of its programs, stakeholder engagement, monitoring and evaluation, fundraising and compliance and people management. Having worked on program implementation in the areas of disability* *rights and health for marginalized people and monitoring, Ketan has professional experience on both sides of the program cycle. He has Masters degree in Political Science (Gold Medallist) and an MBA in Social Entrepreneurship.*

Disha Kapadia-Chinchwadkar *has M.A. in Psychology and MBA (HR) from the University of Mumbai. She also has corporate experience in Human Resources. Currently, she works with the XRCVC, St. Xavier's College, Mumbai on its awareness and advocacy programs.*

KARNA VIDYA FOUNDATION

Empowering Persons with Visual Impairments through Technology

Introduction

Karna Vidya Foundation (KVF) is a not-for-profit registered trust working With Motto ''Empowering Persons with Visual Impairments through Technology. Karna Vidya was started in 1999 as a project by Rotary Club of Madras Coromandel. Karna Vidya - simply means "Learning through Hearing". For people with Visual Impairments, access to gathering knowledge is through their Karna (Ears) assisted by Technology.

Our journey

In 1999, "Karna Vidya Reading Centre" was established. After the successful establishment of the Reading Centre, an urge to do more in the field of academic support led to the setting up of the "Karna Vidya Library" in 2003. Later t was felt that the Persons with Visual Impairments needed a platform to get trained and qualified to get employment in mainstream organizations. This led to the setting up of the "Karna Vidya Technology Centre" in 2013. The centre uses the latest assistive technology training to help the students with Visual Impairments learn and access information. In 2016, all these units were combined under an independent umbrella trust called "KARNA VIDYA FOUNDATION ".

Objectives

- Our primary objective is for EMPOWERING PERSONS WITH VISUAL IMPAIRMENTS THROUGH
- TECHNOLOGY to make them independent and productive citizens.

Services

- Training programmes for college students Training Programme for School students.
- Vocational Services for Job seekers.
- Vocational Services for Entrepreneurs.

- Reading Centre – For assisted learning Library- Physical and digital.
- Advocacy.

Achievements

- Authorized Training Centre of Tamil Nadu Skill Development Corporation
- Awarded the prestigious SIGNIFICANT ACHIEVEMENT PROJECT by Rotary International Recognized by Government of Tamil Nadu as an NGO working for the welfare of Persons with disabilities.
- More than two decades of, providing volunteer reading services for students benefitting over 5000 students.
- Providing digital and physical library with material benefiting over 2000 students.
- Providing technology-based training at school and college level benefitting over 2500 students and professionals.
- More than 50 + awareness camps, counselling sessions, conferences on education, career, technology, digital literacy to students, their parents, and adults across Tamil Nadu.
- More than 100 Candidates have got employed in IT, Banking and Telecom sector. 200+ job seekers have been counseled and facilitated for suitable job roles.

Going forward

- KVF will expand to twenty-five centres by 2025-26 across Tamil Nadu and some neighbouring states for easy access to Visually Impaired school students and Job seekers in the interior parts.
- KVF now seeks to expand its training also to the unschooled and poorly schooled students in local schools, especially in rural areas through Oasis@Schools project by taking education to their doorstep. Most of the parents of visually impaired children at the village level are daily wage earners and it takes enormous effort and sacrifice on their part to bring the children even to the Government Day care centers or inclusive schools. The Krishnagiri district in Tamil Nadu has been chosen to undertake this project.
- KVF will conduct seminars, awareness camps and training programmes for government teachers and special educators, Govt officials etc. to create a better eco-system to understand and serve the needs of the students with visual impairments.
- KVF is expanding its training to the students on curricular and non-curricular content covering STREAM (Science, Technology, Right Living, English, Arts and Maths) subjects. This will lead to more inclusive school education and opening new subjects for the VI students to pursue higher education.
- KVF is setting up a team to actively work with the corporates in doing the design and development of course content in association with skill development corporations and the Corporates

- KVF is expanding its services to cover self-employment, and a team will actively work with Govt agencies and corporates to identify self-employment opportunities. This will include stalls or booths on Metro stations for awareness creation, engagement in addition to self-employment

- KVF is developing a Digital platform for Online education and Engagement. KVF is also building a learning device, the first of its kind, combining audio, tactile and braille elements

- KVF is expanding its E book Publication to include more curricular and extracurricular books for publishing on Bookshare and Sugama Pusthakalay platforms.

- Collaboration with colleges, skills development corporations to provide industry ready resources.

- KVF is planning a scholarship program for the needy students

- KVF proposes to have minivans/buses to reach out to students in remote areas

- KVF is proposing a long-term project of setting up an experience centre/park to give visually impaired students a tactile experience of the world around them. This will be a five-year project and will be set up on a twenty-acre plot in Krishnagiri which there is prima facie go ahead by the district authorities. The design work on the park will be completed in the next year in collaboration with engineering colleges and Universities.

Acknowledgments

KVF is grateful to Rotary Club of Madras Coromandel, Government of Tamil Nadu, CSR sponsors like MINDSPRINT, Titan, Tech Mahindra and Technip, large number of individual donors and partners like Bookshare, Daisy Consortium and Enable India.

Addresses

Training Centre

Fifth Floor, RR Towers 2,

TVK Industrial Estate, Guindy,

Chennai 600 032

Contact:

Office: Mobile: +91 7200254589

Landline: 044 6666 4101

Contact:

Trustee: V Subramaniam + 91984002233:   vsubu2000@yahoo.com

Sasikumar – Programme Head: +919788900794   training@karnavidyafoundation.org

Library

Mandaveli- Door No.1, Rani Annadurai Street, Mandaveli, Chennai 600 028

Contact: Shyla Viswanathan / +91 93810 04365 / shylavish@gmail.com

Website

www.karnavidyafoundation.org